Speaking of Information

Speaking of Information
The Library Juice Quotation Book

Compiled by Rory Litwin
Edited by Martin Wallace
Foreword by Michael Gorman

Library Juice Press
Duluth, Minnesota

Published in 2009 by Library Juice Press
PO Box 3320
Duluth, MN 55803

http://libraryjuicepress.com/

This book is printed on acid-free paper meeting all present ANSI standards for archival preservation.

Quotations included in this book may be from copyrighted works and may appear here under the "fair use" exceptions to U.S. copyright law. The front matter was written in 2008, with copyright held by the respective contributors, and may not be used without permission.

Library of Congress Cataloging-in-Publication Data

Litwin, Rory.
 Speaking of information : the Library juice quotation book / compiled by Rory Litwin ; edited by Martin Wallace ; foreword by Michael Gorman.
    p. cm.
 Summary: "A compilation of quotations originally collected for the 'Quotes of the Week' section of Library Juice, an electronic magazine that dealt with philosophical and political dimensions of librarianship"--Provided by publisher.
 Includes bibliographical references and index.
 ISBN 978-0-9802004-1-6 (acid-free paper)
 1. Library science--Quotations, maxims, etc. 2. Information science--Quotations, maxims, etc. I. Wallace, Martin, 1973- II. Library juice. III. Title.
 PN6084.L52L58 2009
 020--dc22
                                                    2008054713

Contents

Foreword	vii
Preface	ix
Editor's Introduction	xi
Acknowledgments	xiv
On Books and Reading	1
On Libraries	11
Information Technology	21
Information Control	33
Censorship	51
Copyright	59
Data, Information, Knowledge & Other Wisdom	63
Information Overload	73
On Librarians	79
Guardians of History	87
Social Responsibility	99
Neutrality	107
Liberty or Slavery	115
Truth & Lie	119
Secrecy	125
Notes	129
Author Index	147

Foreword

Books of quotations serve many functions. They can entertain, enrich, inform, infuriate, define (by inclusion and exclusion), and/or provide one end of a strand of knowledge to be pursued elsewhere by the enquiring mind. Some quotations are comical, some profound, but a true quotation book is neither a collection of jokes or one-liners on the one hand nor an assemblage of profundities and pomposities on the other. Essentially, every quotation book is an argument in favor of a field of study or one that attempts to influence that field of study. Even the venerable general compendia, such as *The Oxford Book of Quotations*, are arguments, rooted in their times, for a particular way of looking at the canon of literature and thought. The Oxford book of quotations (second edition, revised, 1953) argues that certain authors and certain books belong to the canon to the exclusion of other authors and books and, thus, defines what literature consisted of to its editors. It assigns ten pages to hundreds of quotations from Rudyard Kipling and four lines to two quotations from Robert Frost, thus, placing those authors on a scale of importance in that canon. In much the same way, this book of quotations is an argument for a particular way of looking at libraries, library work, and the great causes of the library profession—intellectual freedom, literacy, social responsibility, etc. *Library Juice* was, inarguably, a progressive publication and the progressive view of libraries and librarianship could be seen in the selection of quotations that began each issue. That shaping of the field could have been seen even if this were simply a reprinting of those quotations in chronological order, but emerges even more strongly in the selection from, and grouping of, those quotations that you will find here. What is librarianship about? The compiler and editor of this book will give you an answer, one that I find compelling, an answer that can be found, at one level, in the contents list and, at another level, in the selections themselves. Fortunately for the reader, the compiler and editor take a broad as well as a progressive view and a stroll through these quotations is one undertaken with an eclectic bunch of companions. It is hard indeed to resist a selection with an index that yields the successive entries "Goering, Hermann," "Goethe, Johann Wolfgang von," and "Goldman, Emma." So, relax, read, enjoy, and prepare to have your view of our profession reinforced, challenged, and/or broadened.

Michael Gorman
Chicago, Illinois
December 2008

Preface

My interest in libraries was initially like a match lighting. I was in my late 20's and sorely needed something to which to devote my energy and my future life. On discovering librarianship, I entered a master's program with an enthusiasm for the world of libraries and librarianship so intense that made me something of an oddball at my school. I started publishing *Library Juice*, the electronic serial wherein I originally compiled the quotations in these pages, in 1998, while I was still a grad student. By 2005, when I stopped publishing *Library Juice* as a standard serial publication and began planning the current blog and book publishing company, the match-head of my passion for libraries had been consumed and the flame was now steady and reliable.

The passage of a few years has given me enough distance from the days when I compiled these quotations to reflect on my selections a little bit. I started each weekly, and then bi-weekly, issue of *Library Juice* with a quotation that I had found in some reading that I had just encountered. I read widely on librarianship and supporting disciplines while a student at San Jose State's School of Library and Information Science, often to the neglect of my coursework (which I found dull and disappointingly bereft of intellectual challenge and professional interest). I read articles from the "library Left" (in *Progressive Librarian* and elsewhere); I read mainstream professional literature; I read literature from the scholarly side of things (like *Library Quarterly*); I read outside of librarianship (sociology, technology) and I became interested in the history of the profession, finding inspiration from works 20, 40, 80 years old and older. In the late 90s and early 2000s, "change" was on everybody's lips (as it is now), and I found it useful and instructive to find out from library history what was indeed new and what was in fact an old thread being spun out into the present. I made many friends out in the profession while a student in library school—some library science faculty and some active librarians—who shared these interests and led me to many of the readings from which I plucked the quotes compiled here.

If I could name one person in the history of libraries whose vision defines the conceptualization of librarianship that underlies the selection of quotations here, however, I would not hesitate to name Jesse Shera. Shera thought broadly about the profession, always seeking to understand what it is that librarians do and where libraries were headed through a process of deep analysis that considered sociological and philosophical perspectives. His primary concern was with the foundations of the profession, in terms of institutions, readers, technology, and society. His *Foundations for Education in Librarianship* gave me my orientation to the profession and its scholarly discipline. Of every person quoted here, it is to him that this book owes the most.

I should also mention that this book is not simply a catalog of every "quote for the week" from Library Juice. Martin Wallace approached his responsibilities as this book's editor with a work ethic that few others would have brought to it. His work in selecting the best quotes, organizing them in themes, verifying them all, sourcing the ones that were not well sourced, and laying the book out graphically, was essential to creating what you now hold in your hands.

Rory Litwin
November 4, 2008
Duluth, MN

Editor's Introduction

I am often asked by my friends, family and non-librarian colleagues, "What exactly do librarians do?" More often than not they seem to have the impression that librarians spend their days actually reading books, interrupted by the occasional patron in need of assistance; they have little understanding of the intellectual labor involved in the smooth operation of libraries; but, I have never had a satisfactory answer for them, for I myself had not experienced or explored the full gamut of library work. My answer is usually a terse statement that includes something about the teaching of database searching, the selection of new materials and the updating of web pages. On a personal scale of my particular position at the University of Maine, I spend a significant amount of time on these very tasks, so I naturally assume that all librarians do too.

In a manner of speaking, editing this book has exposed me to a much more comprehensive understanding of my profession. The work involved in editing *Speaking of Information* demonstrated a marriage of the material and the conceptual aspects of librarianship, in all its myriad facets. On the more down-to-earth, material level, I experienced a microcosm of the labor of librarianship. Each quotation in this book underwent a process of selection, classification, organization and presentation for use, much like the volumes found in a library are.

In order to edit this compilation of quotes, I first had to analytically examine each quotation and extract core meanings. I had to group related quotes together into categories that later became chapters. This was not an easy task because many of the quotations would equally fit into two or more categories and some of them had to be discarded, as they didn't seem to fit at all.

By researching the quotations and their attributions, I exposed myself to a very broad range of philosophy and social activity that has focused on and sprouted from librarianship and the broader study of information, including its relationships to technology, science, literacy, and politics. From this research I could only conclude that librarians are also in the practice of protecting civil liberties, exploring the intersection of technology and society, and are intimately connected to the construction of civilizations itself. Who knew?

Ultimately, working on this project has had a therapeutic effect—intellectually stimulating, challenging, a great learning experience and a true labor of love for my profession.

A Note About Notes

The nature of the Web allows one to quickly and without much thought post a quotation without verifying or correctly citing its source. This leads to a phenomenon of misattributed quotations propagating exponentially across the Web unchecked, and for all practical purposes, impossible to correct. There were a few instances of this phenomenon apparent in the quotations used in the original *Library Juice* "Quote of the Week" from which this book was derived. I even found one example of this phenomenon originating from a 1970s print publication that was misattributed in several other pre-Web print publications.

To the credit of *Library Juice*, and unlike most collections of quotations on the Web, *LJ* usually cited original sources; incorrect attributions were far less frequent than found elsewhere, and were often reliant on secondary sources that one would expect to have reliably cited quotes, such as news publications and authoritative reference works.

Nonetheless, a few mistakes were found, so I have made every effort to research the provenance and establish authenticity of the quotations found in *Speaking of Information*. Suffice to say that all the quotations included in this book are from verifiable primary sources, or found in reputable (while admittedly fallible) secondary sources such as quotations dictionaries. Some quotations originated from a variety of ephemeral sources, such as email lists, speeches, or personal conversations. On these I consulted with Rory Litwin, who had originally compiled the quotes, and he was able to provide exact sources for them. Where possible, I contacted original contributors (authors) for clarification.

Acknowledgments

Several people deserve acknowledgement for helping with this book. Above all I thank Rory Litwin of Library Juice Press for granting me the opportunity to work on this project. Rory has provided support for the publication conceptually, editorially, technically and financially and has shown endless patience and guidance, even after I missed two deadlines for the book's completion.

Second, I thank Mr. Ralph Keyes, author of *The Quote Verifier: Who Said What. Where. And When*. Keyes' book was instrumental to this book in two ways—first, it clarified the origins of several of the quotations included in the compilation; and second, it provided inspiration for conducting the necessary hard work of carefully researching the authenticity of each quotation and attribution. It is by the intellectual labor of scholars such as Mr. Keyes that the historical record and provenance of ideas are not completely lost to oblivion.

Third, I thank members of Radical Reference who assisted in verifying attributions that completely stumped me. Several of the quotations in this book would not have been included if not for their committed (and somewhat anonymous) volunteerism. Thank you jbeek, jenna, lisa, and xarathustra.

Fourth, I need to thank a mysterious colleague at the University of Maine who apparently wishes to remain anonymous. The day after I posted to Radical Reference and the Progressive Librarians Guild a question regarding correct attribution of an elusive George Orwell quotation, I arrived at work to find the book on my desk with the page in the book marked where the quote could be found. There was no note indicating who left the book on my desk, and no one has come forth to claim responsibility for it.

I should also thank each of the contributors and authors of these quotations; those living and those passed. Many of the contributors whom I contacted took time to verify their own quotations and to provide me with primary sources. It was a delight to hear from each of them and to have their permission (and gratitude) for inclusion in this book.

Martin Wallace
October 30, 2008
Orono, Maine

Chapter One:
On Books and Reading

A book is a garden carried in the pocket.

~Arabian proverb[1]

We are too civil to books. For a few golden sentences we will turn over and actually read a volume of four or five hundred pages.

> ~Ralph Waldo Emerson[2]

A man should hear a little music, read a little poetry, and see a fine picture every day of his life, in order that worldly cares may not obliterate the sense of the beautiful which God has implanted in the human soul.

> ~Johann Wolfgang von Goethe[3]

Let us read and let us dance—these two amusements will never do any harm to the world.

> ~Voltaire[4]

Were we to choose our leaders on the basis of their reading experience and not their political programs, there would be much less grief on earth. I believe—not empirically, alas, but only theoretically—that for someone who has read a lot of Dickens to shoot his like in the name of an idea is harder than for someone who has read no Dickens.

~Joseph Brodsky[5]

For years, we've been bludgeoned with the cliche "information is power." But information isn't power. After all, who's got the most information in your neighborhood? Librarians. And they're famous for having no power at all. And who has the most power in your community? Politicians. And they're notorious for being ill-informed.

~From the jacket of Clifford Stoll's *High Tech Heretic: Why Computers Don't Belong in the Classroom*[6]

Chapter One: On Books and Reading

If you don't read much, you really don't know much. You're dangerous.

~Jim Trelease[7]

If information is power, why are the powerful so ill informed?

~Unknown[8]

Books are weapons in the war of ideas.

~Slogan of The Council of Books in Wartime, printed on U.S. Office of War Information posters during WWII[9]

Properly, we should read for power. Man reading should be man intensely alive. The book should be a ball of light in one's hand.

~Ezra Pound[10]

The old idea of the intellectual as the one who speaks truth to power is still an idea worth holding on to. Tyrants fear the truth of books because it's a truth that's in hock to nobody, it's a single artist's unfettered vision of the world. They fear it even more because it's incomplete, because the act of reading completes it, so that the book's truth is slightly different in each reader's different inner world, and these are the true revolutions of literature, these invisible, intimate communions of strangers, these tiny revolutions inside each reader's imagination, and the enemies of the imagination, politburos, ayatollahs, all the different goon squads of gods and power, want to shut these revolutions down, and can't. Not even the author of a book can know exactly what effect his book will have, but good books do have effects, and some of these effects are powerful, and all of them, thank goodness, are impossible to predict in advance.

~Salman Rushdie[11]

Chapter One: On Books and Reading

How many a man has dated a new era in his life from the reading of a book!

~Henry David Thoreau[12]

I have often reflected upon the new vistas that reading opened to me. I knew right there in prison that reading had changed forever the course of my life. As I see it today, the ability to read awoke in me some long dormant craving to be mentally alive.

~Malcolm X[13]

In prison, there were no rifles for training, no stone fortresses from which to shoot. Behind those walls, our rifles were books. And through study, stone by stone we built our fortress, the only one that is invincible: the fortress of ideas.

~Fidel Castro[14]

When I was in prison, I was wrapped up in all those deep books. That Tolstoy crap. People shouldn't read that stuff.

~Mike Tyson[15]

Our modern system of popular Education ... has produced a vast population able to read but unable to distinguish what is worth reading.

~G.M. Trevelyan[16]

There is only one way to read, which is to browse in libraries and bookshops, picking up books that attract you, reading only those, dropping them when they bore you, skipping the parts that drag and never, never reading anything because you feel you ought, or because it is part of a trend or a movement. Remember that the book which bores you when you are twenty or thirty will open doors for you when you are forty or fifty and vice versa. Don't read a book out of its right time for you.

~Doris Lessing[17]

An old writer says that there are four sorts of readers: Sponges, which attract all without distinguishing; Howre-glasses, which receive and powre out as fast; Bagges, which retain the degrees of the spices and let the wine escape; and Sieves, which retain the best only. A man wastes a great many years before he reaches the "sieve" stage.

~Sir William Osler[18]

Chapter One: On Books and Reading

Critics examine the most recurrent words in a book and count them! Look instead for the words the author avoided, those he was close to or unmistakably far from, alien to, or fastidious about, whereas others are not.

~Henri Michaux[19]

I'm a voracious reader. You have to read to survive. People who read for pleasure are wasting their time. Reading isn't fun; it's indispensable.

~Woody Allen[20]

"I read" I say. "I study and read. I bet I've read everything you've read. Don't think I haven't. I consume libraries. I wear out spines and ROM-drives. I do things like get in a taxi and say, 'The library, and step on it.'"

~Hal, in David Foster Wallace's *Infinite Jest*[21]

It does not matter how many books you may have, but whether they are good or not.

~Lucius Annaeus Seneca[22]

Book reading is a solitary and sedentary pursuit, and those who do are cautioned that a book should be used as an integral part of a well-rounded life, including a daily regimen of rigorous physical exercise, rewarding personal relationships, and a sensible low-fat diet. A book should not be used as a substitute or an excuse.

~Garrison Keillor[23]

*Chapter Two:
On Libraries*

I have always imagined that Paradise will be a kind of library.

~Jorge Luis Borges[1]

Chapter Two: On Libraries

We need our libraries open to all, so we can prepare our students for the 21st Century.

~Martin Luther King[2]

A library that's open 24 hours a day—that's my idea of the American Dream.

~Sita Block, Santa Clara County Library patron[3]

When I enter this little library I wonder how I am able to leave it again.

~Marie de Sevigne[4]

You do not really leave a library; if you do what it wants you to do, then you are taking it with you.

~Elie Wiesel[5]

People can lose their lives in libraries. They ought to be warned.

~Saul Bellow[6]

Homer Kelly basked in happiness. He adored libraries, any library, from a closet full of books in a rural town hall to the vast collections of Widener Library in Harvard Yard. To Homer, libraries were holy places like churches, and the priestly librarians a blessed race, a saving remnant in a world of sin. Whenever God grew impatient and decided to destroy the world he remembered the librarians and stayed his hand. At least that was Homer's opinion.

~Jane Langton[7]

Chapter Two: On Libraries

> Libraries are what churches *should* be.
>
> ~rushmc, in a posting to a *Metafilter* thread about libraries[8]

My grandma always said that God made libraries so that people didn't have any excuse to be stupid. Close to everything a human being needed to know was somewhere at the library.

~Jenna Boller, in Joan Bauer's *Rules of the Road*[9]

In my day the library was a wonderful place. ... We didn't have visual aids and didn't have various programs ... it was a sanctuary. ... So I tend to think the library should remain a center of knowledge.

~Norman Mailer[10]

Libraries are reservoirs of strength, grace and wit, reminders of order, calm and continuity, lakes of mental energy, neither warm nor cold, light nor dark. The pleasure they give is steady, unorgastic, reliable, deep and long-lasting.

~Germaine Greer[11]

The Dispensary of the Soul

~Inscription on the library in Thebes, Egypt, c2000 BCE

No place affords a more striking conviction of the vanity of human hopes, than a public library; for who can see the wall crowded on every side by mighty volumes, the works of laborious meditation and accurate inquiry, now scarcely known but by the catalogue, and preserved only to increase the pomp of learning, without considering how many hours have been wasted in vain endeavours, how often imagination has anticipated the praises of futurity, how many statues have risen to the eye of vanity, how many ideal converts have elevated zeal, how often wit has exulted in the eternal infamy of his antagonists, and dogmatism has delighted in the gradual advances of his authority, the immutability of his decrees, and the perpetuity of his power?

~Samuel Johnson[12]

Chapter Two: On Libraries

Libraries are the face of government as it existed before we started hating government and, therefore, ourselves.

~Jennifer Vogel[13]

With a library you are free, not confined by temporary political climates. It is the most democratic of institutions because no one—but no one at all—can tell you what to read and when and how.

~Doris Lessing[14]

There is not such a cradle of democracy upon the earth as the Free Public Library, this republic of letters, where neither rank, office, nor wealth receives the slightest consideration.

~Andrew Carnegie[15]

What a sad want I am in of libraries, of books to gather facts from! Why is there not a Majesty's library in every town? There is a Majesty's jail and gallows in every one.

~Thomas Carlyle[16]

my library was dukedom large enough
~Prospero, in William Shakespeare's *The Tempest*[17]

Thus in an age of specialization, of social fragmentation, the library, like the communication system of which it is a part, can become a great cohesive force at a time when social cohesion is most vital. But unlike the mass media of communication it need not be an instrument for the achievement of conformity. It is, and should remain, the stronghold of individualism. Whereas the mass media, the newspaper, radio, television, are declaratory, the library is interrogative. To the library men come seeking truth, each in his own way for his own ends. In the library the patron is not told what to think or when to think it, but in his search each must discover for himself the thoughts and opinions of others and try to understand them, to appreciate them for what they are, even though he may not share them. The library, then, must be a force for understanding, for cohesion, in a world of antagonisms, conflict, and specialization, but it must be a unifying, not a homogenizing force. The social role of the library is a very complex role and the responsibilities which society, often quite unwittingly, has placed upon it are very heavy. Certainly there is no one library form that can achieve them all; there must be many types of libraries to assume so varied a burden. But there is a unity in the library process as an agent of communication. In the character of that unity lies the key to the dilemma which the library faces today.

~Jesse Shera[18]

Chapter Two: On Libraries

The library is a social institution. The physical space accommodates admirably the human need for people to be in community with other people. People like the library because there are other people there for them to share the space with, talk to, or learn from.

~Maurice J. (Mitch) Freedman[19]

With my library card I am rich. It is my access to the inviting learning world.

~Loretta Jordan,
Washington, D.C. library patron[20]

Libraries will get you through times of no money better than money will get you through times of no libraries.

~Ann Herbert[21]

Whatever the costs of our libraries, the price is cheap compared to that of an ignorant nation.

~Walter Cronkite[22]

My alma mater was books, a good library. ... If I weren't out here every day battling the white man, I could spend the rest of my life reading, just satisfying my curiosity—because you can hardly mention anything I'm not curious about.

~Malcolm X[23]

If truth is beauty, how come no one has their hair done in the library?

~Lily Tomlin[24]

You see, I don't believe that libraries should be drab places where people sit in silence, and that's been the main reason for our policy of employing wild animals as librarians.

~Monty Python's Flying Circus[25]

Chapter Three: Information Technology

Every day, computers are making people easier to use.

~David Temkin[1]

Chapter Three: Information Technology

True teaching and learning are about more than information. Education is based on mentoring, internalization, identification, role-modeling, guidance, and group activity. In these processes, physical proximity plays an important role. Thus, the strength of the future physical university lies less in pure information and more in college as a community. Less in wholesale lecture, and more in individual tutorial. Less in Cyber-U, and more in Goodbye-Chips College. In research, the physical university's strength lies in establishing on-campus archipelagos of specialized islands of excellence that benefit from the complementarity of physical proximity. This requires the active management of priorities. In the validation of information, the university will become more important than ever. As the production of information keeps growing, society requires credible screeners of information, and has entrusted some of that function to universities and its resident experts, not to networks. But to shield the credibility of this function requires universities to be vigilant against creeping self-commercialization and self-censorship.

~Eli M. Noam[2]

Physical separateness can never be overcome by electronics, but only by "conviviality", by "living together" in the most literal physical sense. The physically divided are also the conquered and the Controlled. "True desires"—erotic, gustatory, olfactory, musical, aesthetic, psychic, & spiritual—are best attained in a context of freedom of self and other in physical proximity & mutual aid. Everything else is at best a sort of representation.

~Hakim Bey[3]

Chapter Three: Information Technology

The use of e-mail, online catalogs, the Internet, and cleverly designed home pages that have the look and feel of a modern library have, in a virtual sense, created a situation in which one cannot distinguish the library's presence from that of the Church of Jesus Christ of Latter-Day Saints, Ryder Truck Rental, or Duffy's Tavern in Boalsburg, Pennsylvania.

~Bernard Vavrek[4]

Man is not a machine. ... Although man most certainly processes information, he does not necessarily process it in the way computers do. Computers and men are not species of the same genus. ... However much intelligence computers may attain, now or in the future, theirs must always be an intelligence alien to genuine human problems and concerns.

~Joseph Weizenbaum[5]

Becoming increasingly dominant within librarianship is what might be termed the Techno-Blockbuster Philosophy, which views digital technology as the overriding fact of the future, rendering traditional formats like books, magazines, CDs & videos ultimately superfluous, with a corollary emphasis—for the time being—on conglomerate-published, Madison Avenue hyped "bestsellers," which may be bought in massive quantities to satisfy artificially-created demand.

~Sanford (Sandy) Berman[6]

There is no escaping from ourselves. The human dilemma is as it has always been, and we solve nothing fundamental by cloaking ourselves in technological glory.

~Neil Postman[7]

Librarians persist in sublimating librarianship to the lure of the machine ...

~Jesse Shera[8]

In the place of competencies and commonalities electronic spaces offer swiftly shifting and easily shared particularities. Web spiders, search engines, and software agents are the cyborgian protozoa in an evolutionary scheme that will take us, humans and machines, toward a coevolutionary world of likewise evolving questions. This evolutionary cell-splitting already increasingly takes the form of what I call gritty searches. More cautious creatures are supplanted by more numerous ones. Smoothly constructed searches are increasingly displaced by successive quick approximations that at each turn are cleansed by iterative query refinements, taking place in virtual and actual communities, involving both computational agents and human beings, and resulting in idiosyncratic and dynamic representations of search and searcher alike. To a contemporary reference librarian such searches are liable to signal a loss of clarity. Even when (or especially because) a machine does most of the floundering, these searches seem wastefully spatial, gestural, fuzzy, haphazard, and physical, and thus gritty in the sense that the particularity of an evolving planet and its creatures are gritty. Yet if they herald a loss it is, I think, the cleansing and morphogenetic loss that engenders a newness.

~Michael Joyce[9]

At some crucial moment in the 19th century, the means of production replaced the meaningfulness of the product as a subject of intellectual discourse. Recently, the same thing occurred with technology. What is now of critical moment is information technology (the means of communication), and not the thought communicated. Process has replaced substance.

~Robert Hauptman[10]

I don't think we should be automating information professionals out of business. Quite the contrary, I think we should be giving them a bigger job: reaching out to support the collective cognition of particular communities. This might include systems to support the creation, circulation, and transformation of particular genres of materials. It might include setting up and configuring mailing lists or other, more sophisticated tools for shared thinking. It might include both face-to-face and remote assistance. Distributed alliances of librarians might support specific distributed communities, while comparing notes with one another and sharing tools.

~Phil Agre[11]

Chapter Three: Information Technology

As the circuit supplants the printed page, and as more and more of our communications involve us in network processes—which of their nature plant us in a perpetual present—our perception of history will inevitably alter. Changes in information storage and access are bound to impinge on our historical memory. The depth of field that is our sense of the past is not only a linguistic construct, but is in some essential way represented by the book and the physical accumulation of books in library spaces. In the contemplation of the single volume, or mass of volumes, we form a picture of time past as a growing deposit of sediment; we capture a sense of its depth and dimensionality. Moreover, we meet the past as much in the presentation of words in books of specific vintage as we do in any isolated fact or statistic. The database, useful as it is, expunges this context, this sense of chronology, and admits us to a weightless order in which all information is equally accessible.

~Sven Birkerts[12]

I would venture the opinion that the traditional civil libertarian opposition to the banning of books from school libraries and from school curricula is now largely irrelevant. Such acts of censorship are annoying, of course, and must be opposed. But they are trivial. Even worse, they are distracting, in that they divert civil libertarians from confronting those questions that have to do with the claims of new technology.

~Neil Postman[13]

If you aren't scared, you just don't understand.

~UUNet[14]

Chapter Three: Information Technology

Some futurists continue to promote an all-digital future because there's big consulting money in simplistic projections, and nobody seems to check the track records of futurists. Other technologists and futurists focus on their own needs, desires, and capabilities to the exclusion of all else. They don't read books, so books are dead. They circulate preprint journal articles and consider magazines beneath contempt, so periodicals are dead. They don't use public libraries, so neither does anyone else. Based on the articles and books I've seen, most technologists are essentially unaware of public libraries.

~Walt Crawford[15]

There is more to life than increasing its speed.

~Gandhi[16]

The presumed close connection among information, reason, and usefulness began to lose its legitimacy toward the mid-nineteenth century with the invention of the telegraph. Prior to the telegraph, information could be moved only as fast as a train could travel; about thirty-five miles per hour. Prior to the telegraph, information was sought as part of the process of understanding and solving particular problems. Prior to the telegraph, information tended to be of local interest. Telegraphy changed all of this, and instigated the second stage of the information revolution. The telegraph removed space as an inevitable constraint on the movement of information, and, for the first time, transportation and communication were disengaged from each other. In the United States, the telegraph erased state lines, collapsed regions, and, by wrapping the continent in an information grid, created the possibility of a unified nation-state. But more than this, telegraphy created the idea of context-free information—that is, the idea that the value of information need not be tied to any function it might serve in social and political decision-making and action. The telegraph made information into a commodity, a "thing" that could be bought and sold irrespective of uses or meanings.

~Neil Postman[17]

Chapter Four: Information Control

Question Managerial Prerogatives.

~Sandy Berman[1]

Chapter Four: Information Control

In truth, American libraries and the profession of librarianship are confronted with a structural transformation in the overall economy. It is nothing less than thorough privatization of the information function. The production, processing, storing and transmission of information have been scooped up into private, for-profit hands. Social sources and repositories of information have been taken over for commercial use and benefit. It is not because American libraries and library schools have fallen behind in the mastery of the new information technology that their existence increasingly is called into question. It is their bedrock principles and long-term practices that collide with the realities of today's corporate-centered and market-driven economy. The extent to which librarians insist on free and untrammeled access to information, 'unrestricted by administrative barriers, geography, ability to pay or format,' they will be treated by the privatizers as backward-looking, if not obsolete, irrelevant, and unrealistic.

The technology issue, therefore, is merely a screen behind which a far-reaching and socially regressive institutional change has occurred. The focus on technology also serves to delude many, librarians included, that the new means to achieve status and respect is to concentrate on the machinery of information, production, and transmission. When and if this focus turns rigidly exclusive, wittingly or not, the social basis of the profession and the needs of the majority of people are left unattended.

~Herbert Schiller[2]

The life of the man from Hennepin County has the resonance of the heroes in Raymond Carver's short stories, or the individuals who people Sherwood Anderson's America. There is such a close integration of style and sincerity in Sandy's life and his work that he is a modern day eccentric who, without the slightest hesitation, refuses to be anyone but himself. Who is the persona? The quickest way to discover the answer is to turn to his writings, and particularly this collection. If anything characterizes his work it is high ideals. ... The difficulty is that high ideals rarely make for high drama. Sandy may well be the exception. He takes on the outside world with such vigor that his sense of outrage, often tempered with satire and wit, gives anyone with a sense of the ridiculous (and the sublime) pause.

~Bill Katz[3]

I guess that what keeps me in librarianship, even though it has at times been extremely frustrating and even perilous, is a sort of compulsion to share, particularly ideas and information. That accounts for the kind of networking activity which I confess transcends just library colleagues and spills over into the local and even national community. On discovering a piece of solid information that I suspect would interest, say, a small press person or somebody in a particular movement group, or a "new word" collector, I simply find myself unable to suppress the instinct, the impulse, to get it to that person. So this compulsion results in a kind of pro-active, selective dissemination of information, except some would claim that maybe it's not so selective.

~Sandy Berman[4]

Hennepin [County Library] is in the process of shutting down the unique, progressive, socially sensitive and, most importantly, user-oriented cataloging that Sandy [Berman] has been doing since 1973. Hennepin is building up a case to fire him for speaking against automatic acceptance of LC names, and probably in the not-too-distant future, ditto on the LC subject headings and the overall LC cataloging record.

~Mitch Freedman[5]

Since the very usage of language in our culture is defined and expressed via centralized sources of distribution such as television and radio, or as in this case—by LC subject headings, it becomes increasingly difficult to even frame the nature of the debate when the very words which define these inter-relationships and avenues of power have been expunged from the public vocabulary by the purveyors of our common culture, e.g. big business and media conglomerates and by extension, their lackeys, state and federal government, of which LC is clearly a part.

~Peter McDonald[6]

What seemed to me to be at stake at this time was a kind of censorship by effect, at the very source, where decisions are made as to what is identified as news, what information is chosen for dissemination, what ideas and views are considered acceptable, or desirable, to publish and disseminate. And the source was shrinking. Open censorship can be fought openly, and often successfully. But, how can librarians assure the broadest representation of information, opinions, and creative expression in the face of the growing concentration of ownership of communication channels?

~Zoia Horn[7]

Chapter Four: Information Control

The eternal conflict of good and the best with bad and the worst is on. The librarian must be the librarian militant before he can be the librarian triumphant. At the end of another century, when a conference like this is held, our descendants will look back with wonder to find that we have so long been satisfied to leave the control of the all-pervading, all-influencing newspaper in the hands of people who have behind them no motive better that 'the almighty dollar.'

~Melvil Dewey[8]

Model, organize and strategize ways to operate libraries more creatively and free from coercion.

~Chris Dodge[9]

We're one of the most respected and even venerated places in communities. People know that they're going to get pretty objective information and they're not going to be subjected to commercialism.

~Carla Hayden[10]

... and remember, if you can't find it in the library catalog, it looks like it isn't real or never happened.

~Sandy Berman[11]

It ... appears that the late Empire had strong political misgivings about the extension of libraries to the "popular" classes. In April 1864, Interior Minister Paul Boudet dispatched a circular marked "confidential" to department prefects. The circular recalled that in the last two years, private associations like the Société Franklin had "instituted in various places in the Empire popular libraries, whose object is to promote the reading of books particularly destined for the working class."

~Lara Jennifer Moore[12]

I thank God there are no free schools nor printing; and I hope we shall not have [them] these [next] hundred years; for learning has brought disobedience, and heresy, and sects into the world, and printing has divulged them and libels against the best government. God keep us from both!

~Sir William Berkeley[13]

It is of great importance that the general public be given the opportunity to experience, consciously and intelligently, the efforts and results of scientific research. It is not sufficient that each result be taken up, elaborated, and applied by few specialists in the field. Restricting the body of knowledge to a small group deadens the philosophical spirit of a people and leads to spiritual poverty.

~Albert Einstein[14]

How could our precious nation have become so uncharacteristically vulnerable to such an effective use of fear to manipulate our politics? What happened? For one thing there's been a dramatic change in the nature of what the philosopher Jürgen Habermas has described as the structure of the public forum—the way our political discourse takes place. It no longer operates as it once did. It is simply no longer as accessible to the vigorous and free exchange of ideas from individuals in the way those ideas were freely and vigorously exchanged during the period of our founding.

~Al Gore[15]

The phrase, 'the free marketplace of ideas' does not refer to the market value of each idea. On the contrary, what it means is that ideas should have a chance to be put to the public, to be expressed and argued fully, and not in soundbites.

~Andre Schiffrin[16]

Perhaps this is an obvious point, but the democratic postulate is that the media are independent and committed to discovering and reporting the truth, and that they do not merely reflect the world as powerful groups wish it to be perceived. Leaders of the media claim that their news choices rest on unbiased professional and objective criteria, and they have support for this contention in the intellectual community. If, however, the powerful are able to fix the premises of discourse, to decide what the general populace is allowed to see, hear, and think about, and to "manage" public opinion by regular propaganda campaigns, the standard view of how the system works is at serious odds with reality.

~Noam Chomsky and Edward S. Herman[17]

It would be a serious intellectual mistake to confuse information that functions as entertainment with actual, or knowledge-based, information. It would be a mistake as well to simply ignore the cognitive implications of information processing as entertainment. Real information, such as who controls wealth and property in the United States, why prison building outdistances school construction, or comparative rates of upward and downward mobility, is as difficult to locate as it ever was and must be culled from the kinds of books and journals not featured and sometimes not even carried by the megabookstore at the strip mall or reported on by television features.

~Joseph Urgo[18]

Chapter Four: Information Control

The twentieth century has been characterized by three developments of great political importance: the growth of democracy, the growth of corporate power, and the growth of corporate propaganda as a means of protecting corporate power against democracy.

~Alex Carey[19]

An oligarchy of private capital ... cannot be effectively checked even by a democratically organized political society [because] under existing conditions, private capitalists inevitably control, directly or indirectly, the main sources of information. It is thus extremely difficult, and indeed in most cases quite impossible, for the individual citizen to come to objective conclusions and to make intelligent use of his political rights.

~Albert Einstein[20]

The corporate grip on opinion in the United States is one of the wonders of the Western world. No First World country has ever managed to eliminate so entirely from its media all objectivity—much less dissent.

~Gore Vidal[21]

Why of course the *people* don't want war. Why should some poor slob on a farm want to risk his life in a war when the best he can get out of it is to come back to his farm in one piece? Naturally the common people don't want war: neither in Russia, nor in England, nor for that matter in Germany. That is understood. But, after all, it is the leaders of the country who determine the policy and it is always a simple matter to drag the people along, whether it is a democracy, or a fascist dictatorship, or a parliament, or a communist dictatorship. ... Voice or no voice, the people can always be brought to the bidding of the leaders. That is easy. All you have to do is tell them they are being attacked, and denounce the peacemakers for lack of patriotism and exposing the country to danger. It works the same in any country.

~Hermann Goering[22]

Chapter Four: Information Control

It is arguable that the success of business propaganda in persuading us, for so long, that we are free from propaganda is one of the most significant propaganda achievements of the twentieth century.

~Alex Carey[23]

This is the most information intensive war you can imagine. ... We're going to lie about things.

~Unnamed military officer involved in planning the response to the World Trade Center attack[24.]

Perhaps it is a universal truth that the loss of liberty at home is to be charged to the provisions against danger, real or pretended, from abroad.

~James Madison[25]

For truth is rightly named the daughter of time, not of authority.

~Francis Bacon[26]

If I hear 'God Bless America' one more time I think I'm going to puke.

~Anonymous friend of the publisher

The third question, freedom, may be the most fundamental of the questions raised by the information explosion. Can man be free when his encounters with the media are dominated by the engineered response? Can he be free when his culture becomes a kind of propaganda system, when values and concepts are flashed at him so frequently that they are inescapable? Can he become free when the alternatives for his life are shown in increasingly limited ways, so that from childhood he is encouraged to think only in certain terms about what is possible and which routes can be followed successfully?

Freedom may be God's greatest gift to man; it is also something that man achieves, rather than begins with. Obviously, there are different kinds of freedom; the option to choose between brands of cereal at the store is different from the freedom to challenge someone in a ticklish, possible threatening situation. The freedom to believe in what you choose to believe in, to select and fight for a cause, emerges only from mature minds and emotions which allow us to recognize the difference between true and false freedoms.

~William Kuhns[27]

Chapter Four: Information Control

A public that hears only praise and no criticism will predictably answer 'yes' to pollsters who ask whether the President is doing a good job.

~Mark Weisbrot[28]

If you can find something everyone agrees on, it's wrong.

~Morris (Mo) Udall[29]

Whenever you find yourself on the side of the majority, it's time to pause and reflect.

~Mark Twain[30]

The press, which is mostly controlled by vested interests, has an excessive influence on public opinion.

~Albert Einstein[31]

Independent presses are the mainstream. The work they publish is not from the margins of the reading public but from its center.

~Laura Moriarty[32]

Any dictator would admire the uniformity and obedience of the [U.S.] media.

~Noam Chomsky[33]

It is particularly of concern that members of the Executive Committee of Correspondents who have been delegated fiduciary power by Congress to pass on the qualifications of persons entitled to press credentials, are themselves private publishers and journalists with a direct competitive interest in the subject matter of their duties.

~Vigdor Schreibman[34]

I dream of a zine that startles me. I am amazed at how similar in format many zines are to their mass media counterparts. It's not enough to just take a different position than Newsweek. How about questioning the validity of any position at all? The fundamental assumption of nearly all publications available today is that there is a right and a wrong, and this writer knows which is which. Come on! Truth is a figment. All things change. When a zine professes certainty about who should be president or what we should do with murderers, I am often frustrated. I am not reading to find out what I ought to believe; I don't want to be converted. I'd like to see more people admitting their confusion, exploring the truly ambiguous nature of nearly every important issue in modern consciousness.

~E. Persimmon[35]

I can't have information I know would be of interest to someone and not share it.

~Sandy Berman[36]

Chapter Five: Censorship

Whoever would overthrow the liberty of a nation must begin by subduing the freeness of speech.

~John Trenchard and Thomas Gordon[1]

Chapter Five: Censorship

The vast number of titles that are published each year—all of them are to the good, even if some of them may annoy or even repel us for a time. For none of us would trade freedom of expression and of ideas for the narrowness of the public censor. America is a free market for people who have something to say, and need not fear to say it.

~Hubert H. Humphrey[2]

We are not afraid to entrust the American people with unpleasant facts, foreign ideas, alien philosophies, and competitive values. For a nation that is afraid to let its people judge the truth and falsehood in an open market is a nation that is afraid of its people.

~John F. Kennedy[3]

It seems to me that libraries stand, above all, for the enlightened and rational notion that human beings are improved by the acquisition of knowledge and information and that no bar should be placed in their way. We stand for the individual human being pursuing whatever avenues of enquiry she or he wishes. We also stand for rationalism as the basis for all of our policies and procedures in libraries. Librarianship is a supremely rational profession and should resist the forces of irrationalism both external and internal.

~Michael Gorman[4]

Both Catholic and Anglican hold the city by the throat, and mould the habits and opinions of the people of Toronto. No book or lecture can have any success that does not have the stamp of approval of the churches. Perhaps you will understand the whole situation when I tell you that the librarian of the public library ... declared: "No, we do not censor books, we simply do not get them." He certainly spoke the truth.

~Emma Goldman[5]

Chapter Five: Censorship

I have never met a public librarian who approved of censorship or one who failed to practice it in some measure.

~Leon Carnovsky[6]

I congratulate you for having opened the doors of libraries and schools to pornographic literature.

~Larry Flynt to Ken Starr, in an invitation to join the staff of *Hustler* magazine[7]

The books that the world calls immoral are the books that show the world its own shame.

~Lord Harry, in Oscar Wilde's *The Picture of Dorian Gray*[8]

Censorship is to art what lynching is to justice.
~Henry Louis Gates Jr.[9]

A censor is a man who knows more than he thinks you ought to.

~Dr. Laurence J. Peter[10]

As to the evil which results from a censorship, it is impossible to measure it, for it is impossible to tell where it ends.

~Jeremy Bentham[11]

Bury the books and you bury the dream ever so deeply. Mediocrity is the chief villain who carries the spade and digs so ever efficiently. Bury the books and you kill the future.

~Anonymous

This is one of those critical moments in history, and I did not want to look back and regret not having said something.

~Aaron McGruder, author of *The Boondocks* newspaper cartoon, explaining why the strip has expressed anti-war, pro-civil liberty opinions in the weeks following 9-11[12]

What is freedom of expression? Without the freedom to offend, it ceases to exist.

~Salman Rushdie[13]

Intellectual Freedom without Alternative Ideas is a Sham.

~Charles Willett[14]

Chapter Five: Censorship

A central lesson of science is that to understand complex issues (or even simple ones), we must try to free our minds of dogma and to guarantee the freedom to publish, to contradict, and to experiment. Arguments from authority are unacceptable.

~Carl Sagan[15]

The right of freedom of speech and press includes not only the right to utter or to print, but the right to distribute, the right to receive, [and] the right to read ...

~U.S. Supreme Court, *Griswold v. Connecticut,* 1965[16]

Free thought, necessarily involving freedom of speech & press, I may tersely define thus: no opinion a law—no opinion a crime.

~Alexander Berkman[17]

If mankind minus one were of one opinion, then mankind is no more justified in silencing the one than the one—if he had the power—would be justified in silencing mankind.

~John Stuart Mill[18]

Congress shall make no law abridging the freedom of sXXXch, or the right of the people peaceably to XXXemble, and to peXXXion the government for a redress of grievances.

~The First Amendment according to XStop Internet Filtering Software[19]

Most of these (filtering) horror stories are taking place in schools. Why? Because so many have insisted so hard that school libraries are different. They act in loco parentis. Who, I'd like to know, is acting in loco parentis for those parents who *don't* want their kids to have only filtered access? I've asked that question, and haven't gotten an answer yet. When we ask questions about the welfare of all kids, the issues seem to quickly turn to questions of legal liability, as if what's best for kids and whether or not somebody might sue the school are necessarily the same thing all the time.

~Melora Ranney Norman[20]

Filtering advocates are caught in a bind. On the one hand, they believe they can keep children pure by protecting them from the evil that is on the internet. On the other hand, they assume that children are naturally corrupt in needing protection from their own 'natural curiosity.' This curiosity, unfettered in the public library that doesn't filter the internet, will then foil the purity of their children.

~Lucy Barber[21]

Chapter Six: Copyright

I don't think we cut into their movie profits last year.

~Patric Parker, attorney representing the Genesee District Library, whose use of a "Book Mouse" mascot was challenged by Disney for trademark infringement[1]

Chapter Six: Copyright

To some degree, our professional lives depend on copyright. If we allow publishers to restrict our rights to the information we have purchased so completely that we are unable to provide basic library services, we will have failed in our ability to fulfill our missions. Widespread civil disobedience may be our only ethical option.

~Roy Tennant[2]

I am a critic of copyright in the same way that I am a critic of the United States Government: I criticize it because I love it.

~Siva Vaidhyanathan[3]

Talking about the information commons helps bring into focus diverse phenomena that are otherwise fuzzy or thought to be inconsequential, such as the role of the public domain in enabling creativity. It helps us revisit the premises of copyright law and reveal how some of its assumptions may be empirically questionable in the digital age. For example, it turns out that copyright and contracts are not the only ways to elicit or distribute valuable knowledge in the digital age. Why can't public policy reflect this fact?

~David Bollier[4]

That ideas should freely spread over the globe, for the mortal and mutual instruction of man, and improvement of his condition, seems to have been peculiarly and benevolently designed by nature, when she made them, like fire, expansible over all space, without lessening their density at any point, and like the air in which we breathe, move, and have our physical being, incapable of confinement, or exclusive appropriation.

~Thomas Jefferson[5]

Chapter Seven: Data, Information, Knowledge & Other Wisdom

A word after a word after a word is power.

~Margaret Atwood[1]

Chapter Seven: Data, Information, Knowledge & Other Wisdom

The computer is here to stay, therefore *it* must be made to adapt to the librarians' problems and needs. It must be kept in its proper place as a tool and a slave, or we will become sorcerer's apprentices, with data data everywhere and not a thought to think.

~Jesse Shera[2]

Information is the gunpowder of the mind.

~Neil Postman[3]

Information can tell us everything. It has all the answers. But they are answers to questions we have not asked, and which doubtless don't even arise.

~Jean Baudrillard[4]

The more we try to get a grip on information, the more it slips through our fingers like a ghost. Information, in fact, is the ghost of meaning and our society's worship of the ghost signals a continuing loss of meaning.

~Stephen L. Talbot[5]

The fragmentation of rational knowledge in the postmodern world has produced a focus on information that is unaware of its history.

~Marcus Breen[6]

It's no exaggeration to say that in the information age, texts aren't read, they're searched. But, as Heraclitus said, "If you do not expect the unexpected, you will not find it." To search a text instead of reading it is to renounce its capacity to surprise us, to make of the text more than ever before a tool, and to restrict its range of implication and suggestion to the ends we assign it.

~Chris Fujiwara[7]

We believe information can even be stored and then, later on, retrieved: witness the library, which is commonly regarded as an information storage and retrieval system. In this, however, we are mistaken. A library may store books, microfiches, documents, films, slides, and catalogues but it cannot store information. One can turn a library upside down: no information will come out. The only way one can obtain information from a library is to look at those books, microfiches, documents, slides, etc.

~Heinz von Foerster[8]

All of the books in the world contain no more information than is broadcast as video in a single large American city in a single year. Not all bits have equal value.

~Carl Sagan[9]

It is a very sad thing that nowadays there is so little useless information.

~Oscar Wilde[10]

Life happens too fast for you ever to think about it. If you could just persuade people of this, but they insist on amassing information.

~Kurt Vonnegut[11]

It's significant that we call it the Information Age. We don't talk about the Knowledge Age.

~James Billington[12]

Knowledge is the sculpture chiseled from the stone mass of information, as understanding is chiseled of knowledge, and wisdom of understanding.

~Francis Morrone[13]

"No sooner," says Boswell, "had we made our bow to Mr. Cambridge, in his library, than Johnson ran eagerly to one side of the room, intent on poring over the backs of the books. Sir Joshua observed (aside) 'He runs to the books, as I do to the pictures: but I have the advantage. I can see much more of the pictures than he can of the books.' Mr. Cambridge, upon this, politely said, 'Dr. Johnson, I am going, with your pardon, to accuse myself, for I have the same custom which I perceive you have. But it seems odd that one should have such a desire to look at the backs of books.' Johnson, ever ready for contest, instantly started from his reverie, wheeled about, and answered, 'Sir, the reason is very plain. Knowledge is of two kinds. We know a subject ourselves, or we know where we can find information upon it. When we enquire into any subject, the first thing we have to do is to know what books have treated of it.'"

~A conversation between Samuel Johnson, James Boswell, Sir Joshua Reynolds and the poet Cambridge[14]

Chapter Seven: Data, Information, Knowledge & Other Wisdom

I venture to suggest that we are in the middle of a conceptual revolution rather than an electronic revolution: by which I mean that the electronic communication revolution facilitates the exchange of messages, data, and information. More people can be contacted more frequently with more messages and more information than in the past; but the real revolution is conceptual, and involves the way in which we view information: we are now much more concerned about its quality, application, and usefulness than we were just a few years ago.

~Michael Brittain[15]

To create a new culture does not only mean to make original discoveries on an individual basis. It also and especially means to critically popularize already discovered truths, make them, so to speak, social, therefore give them the consistency of basis for vital actions, make them coordinating elements of intellectual and social relevance.

~Antonio Gramsci[16]

We must not confuse the thrill of acquiring or distributing information quickly with the more daunting task of converting it into knowledge and wisdom.

~*Principles of Technorealism*, Principle 4[17]

If you have knowledge, let others light their candles in it.

~Margaret Fuller[18]

We have an obligation to communicate. Here, we take the time to talk with one another ... and to listen. We believe that information is meant to move and that information moves people.

~Enron's last published annual report[19]

The art of research is the ability to look at the details, and see the passion.

~Daryl Zero, in Jake Kasdan's *The Zero Effect*[20]

When a book and a head collide and there is a hollow sound, is it always from the book?

~Georg Lichtenberg[21]

Remember, Information is not knowledge; Knowledge is not Wisdom; Wisdom is not truth; Truth is not beauty; Beauty is not love; Love is not music; Music is the best.

~Frank Zappa[22]

Chapter Eight: Information Overload

Everybody gets so much information all day long that they lose their common sense.

~Gertrude Stein[1]

Chapter Eight: Information Overload

One distinguishing feature of contemporary culture in America is that information is consumed for diversion rather than for consequential purposes. Paradoxically, in other words, information of all kinds is processed as low-level cognitive distraction, a form of mass entertainment. The collapsing of news, data, broadcast, and leisure media has resulted in an entertainment culture where the act of consuming information is as diversionary as watching a variety show or a situation comedy. ... The simple term "information" may no longer be adequate to describe the spectrum of input available to human beings in their capacities as data processors.

~Joseph Urgo[2]

What information consumes is rather obvious: it consumes the attention of its recipients. Hence, a wealth of information creates a poverty of attention and a need to allocate that attention efficiently among the overabundance of information sources that might consume it.

~Herbert Simon[3]

The only drawback I can imagine to this system is that the potential combinations are so tantalizing, and so fun to explore, that it's hard to imagine having time left for actually reading any of these books. But that's the price you pay for progress.

~Steven Johnson[4]

You don't have to burn books to destroy a culture. Just get people to stop reading them.

~Ray Bradbury[5]

Who of us does not recognize that the life we live, however larded with brave talk about values and thought and ideals, is not actually a life dedicated to immersion in the endless torrent of images, songs, sounds and stories?

~Todd Gitlin[6]

Information networks straddle the world. Nothing remains concealed. But the sheer volume of information dissolves the information. We are unable to take it all in.

~Günther Grass[7]

It [The Internet] is inherently destructive of memory. You think you're getting lots more [information] until you've found out you've made a bargain with the Devil. You've slowly mutated, and have become an extension of the machine.

~James Billington[8]

They've just done a study at the University of Berkeley, California. ... If they took all the new information that's produced in a year and put it on floppy disks and stacked them one on top of the other, it would go 200 million miles into the sky! ... Is that a sign here? Jesus is surely coming!!

~Jack Van Impe[9]

Chapter Nine: On Librarians

The most important asset of any library goes home at night—the library staff.

~Timothy Healy[1]

In early days, I tried not to give librarians any trouble, which was where I made my primary mistake. Librarians like to be given trouble; they exist for it, they are geared to it. For the location of a mislaid volume, an uncatalogued item, your good librarian has a ferret's nose. Give her a scent and she jumps the leash, her eye bright with battle.

~Catherine Drinker Bowen[2]

Librarians ... possess a vast store of politeness. These are people who get asked regularly the dumbest questions on God's green earth. These people tolerate every kind of crank and eccentric and mouth-breather there is.

~Garrison Keillor as Lefty, in *A Prarie Home Companion*[3]

The extreme stereotype of the dowdy librarian with hair in a bun, glasses, a companion cat, and a penchant for the quiet refuge of scholarship, will soon give way to the new extreme of a hot, young infoseeker with an ethnic background who fixes and finds digital things, creates and advises on electronic experiences, mediates at high vortexes, and crusades for the endangered planet and a spiritual life.

~Elizabeth Martinez[4]

When you take 'Personnel Issues in Information Management,' you learn how to supervise library employees, not how to be one. When you take 'Library Administration,' you would do well to remember that you are the one who is being administered, at least in the beginning and probably for a long time ... the program of instruction leads you to believe (in a twist on the old Huey Long boast, 'Every Man a King'): 'Every Librarian a Supervisor.' Now, common sense indicates that this will not be the case. Libraries are hierarchical. To suggest that each new group of graduates will soon be Supervisors is not based in reality. ... So prepare yourself, learn about unions, 'the folks that brought you the weekend' ...

~James Danky[5]

Librarians would do well to remember *Moses* or *Pieta* and think somewhat less frequently of Shannon and Weaver.

~Jesse Shera[6]

Michael Moore: I really didn't realize the librarians were, you know, such a dangerous group.
Buzzflash: Subversive.
Michael Moore: They are subversive. You think they're just sitting there at the desk, all quiet and everything. They're like plotting the revolution, man. I wouldn't mess with them.[7]

Perhaps the two most valuable and satisfactory products of American civilization are the librarian on the one hand and the cocktail in the other. I will not attempt ... the delicate question of deciding which is best, but I am given to understand that some of us have sampled both and found them both equally satisfactory and equally stimulating.

~Louis Stanley Jast[8]

What can I say? Librarians rule.
~Regis Philbin[9]

Of all the professions, librarianship is probably the most derivative and synthetic, is the most dependent upon the more formal disciplines for its own theoretical structure and its corpus of practice. In the past librarians have been disposed to view this characteristic as a fundamental weakness, and it has therefore generated a considerable feeling of professional inferiority. Yet this very quality has given librarianship a uniquely strategic position of leadership in the integration of human knowledge, and it could make of librarianship a great unifying force, not only in the world of scholarship, but also throughout all human life.

~Jesse Shera[10]

> Some say that, after all, his learning is not so great;
> The learned allow him but librarian's state;
> And yet in sober truth it must be said
> All go to him for flour to make their bread.

~Antonio Magliabecchi[11]

The librarian's mission should be, not like up to now, a mere handling of the book as an object, but rather a know how (*mise au point*) of the book as a vital function.

~José Ortega y Gasset[12]

They know the information and how to use it. They know about us kids and how to teach us to use it, too! We need school librarians! Please do whatever you can to protect their positions in our schools.

~Derek Maraszek[13]

Business equates information with profit. Librarians must equate information with understanding. The role of the librarian is to distinguish between data and information, between facts and knowledge, and to be concerned not only with the 'what' and the 'how' but also with the 'why.'

~Patricia Glass Schuman[14]

I'm looking forward to it. You never know. She could become a librarian.

~Madonna, on the prospects of her young daughter, Lourdes, rebelling against her[15]

There's no type of assault quite like that of a limp female librarian: it chills the bones.

~troutfishing[16]

Watch out for those librarians—they'll shush you back to the Stone Age.

~David Grenier[17]

Ah, I love the smell of desperate librarian in the morning.

~Principal Snyder to Mr. Giles, the librarian, in *Buffy the Vampire Slayer*[18]

Happiness is a warm librarian.

~Derek de Solla Price, commenting on library automation[19]

Chapter Ten:
Guardians of History

The struggle of man against power is the struggle of memory against forgetting.

~Mirek, in Milan Kundera's *Book of Laughter and Forgetting*[1]

Chapter Ten: Guardians of History

If large numbers of people believe in freedom of speech, there will be freedom of speech even if the law forbids it. But if public opinion is sluggish, inconvenient minorities will be persecuted, even if laws exist to protect them.

~George Orwell[2]

Librarians see themselves as the guardians of the First Amendment. You got a thousand Mother Joneses at the barricades! I love the librarians, and I am grateful for them!

~Michael Moore[3]

The strength of the Constitution lies entirely in the determination of each citizen to defend it. Only if every single citizen feels duty bound to do his share in this defense are the constitutional rights secure.

~Albert Einstein[4]

Out of the stacks and into the streets! ... Librarians empower people!

~Gary Klein, marching with ALA members at the 1990 Chicago gay pride parade[5].

Many librarians ... work valiantly, sometimes successfully, in the democratic tradition, defending the general social good. Their efforts are part of a larger democratic struggle that is not going well at this time. Alongside besieged public schools and public libraries are other organizations and institutions with democratic objectives and agendas that are also being swamped by technological, financial, and political pressures of the voracious market economy.

~Herbert Schiller[6]

It is especially the narrowing of the range of public discourse in a market-dominated information industry that requires vigilant librarians who recognize that libraries in a corporate sense symbolize the totality of human knowledge in all modes of knowing. As consumers of information products, library systems could, for example, use their collective purchasing power to remain critical of the ethical consequences of convergence and concentration industry trends for their collection and interpretive functions.

~Archie L. Dick[7]

Chapter Ten: Guardians of History

There's no question these are difficult economic times, but the State Library has survived worse. World War II, the Great Depression, the Boeing bust, and the recessions of the early '80s and '90s all left Washington in financially dire straights. We didn't close the library doors then and we shouldn't now. Since 1853, the State Library has helped improve the quality of life in Washington. It has given us an accurate account of history—good, bad, or indifferent—and stopped us from reliving our mistakes. No one alive today can say with certainty which aspects of history will be most important to future generations. For them, we must fulfill our obligation and preserve our legacy to the very best of our ability.

> ~Washington Secretary of State Sam Reed supporting a plan to have his office take over the State Library.[8]

Today, as the United States appears to become ever more conservative and to retreat from the values of pluralistic democracy on which American librarianship's intellectual freedom ideology is grounded, the American library profession, which historically has embraced the dominant ideology, may be faced with more fundamental choices concerning its very identity than ever before.

~Louise S. Robbins[9]

Creating an un-McDonaldized culture in the library is much easier when the library has un-McDonaldized librarians. These individuals can be actively recruited by going beyond the standard requirement of an ALA-accredited MLS, an affinity for technology, knowledge of a foreign language, or other conventional criteria. Asking a candidate for evidence of creativity, whether in terms of unusual projects undertaken or a bold vision of the future, could be one way to gauge a person's potential.

~Brian Quinn[10]

Chapter Ten: Guardians of History

It would seem impossible in a year such as the past year has been with its overturnings and upheavals, not only of material things but of ideals and of what had seemed moral certainties, that we should spend the time of our annual meeting in the discussion of small or esoteric questions. These crises in life show us the littleness of little things, the subserviency of technique; make us feel through the pull of events our connection with the rest of the world, and even with the universe; take us out of our professional selves and make us conscious of more inclusive selves. And they make us see, as perhaps even we have not seen before, that our profession has a not insignificant part to play in world matters. Hence we have chosen as our general theme for the conference, "THE PUBLIC LIBRARY AND DEMOCRACY.

~Mary Wright Plummer[11]

If we are to violate the Constitution, will the people submit to our unauthorized acts? Sir, they ought not to submit; they would deserve the chains that these measures are forging for them. The country will swarm with informers, spies, delators and all the odious reptile tribe that breed in the sunshine of a despotic power. ... the hours of the most unsuspected confidence, the intimacies of friendship, or the recesses of domestic retirement afford no security. The companion whom you most trust, the friend in whom you must confide, the domestic who waits in your chamber, all are tempted to betray your imprudent or unguarded follies; to misrepresent your words; to convey them, distorted by calumny, to the secret tribunal where jealousy presides where fear officiates as accuser and suspicion is the only evidence that is heard. ... Do not let us be told, Sir, that we excite a fervour against foreign aggression only to establish a tyranny at home; that ... we are absurd enough to call ourselves 'free and enlightened' while we advocate principles that would have disgraced the age of Gothic barbarity and establish a code compared to which the ordeal is wise and the trial by battle is merciful and just.

~Edward Livingston[12]

The people of every country are the only guardians of their own rights, and are the only instruments which can be used for their destruction. And certainly they would never consent to be so used were they not deceived. To avoid this, they should be instructed to a certain degree. I have often thought that nothing would do more extensive good at a small expense than the establishment of a small circulating library in every county, to consist of a few well-chosen books, to be lent to the people of the county, under such regulations as would secure their safe return in due time. These should be such as would give them a general view of other history, and particular view of that of their own country, a tolerable knowledge of Geography, the elements of Natural Philosophy, of Agriculture and Mechanics.

~Thomas Jefferson[13]

Auto-da-Fe had left me ravaged. I could not forgive myself for burning the books. ... I felt that I had sacrificed not only my own books but also those of the whole world, the books of all religions, all thinkers, all Eastern literatures, and those of the Western literatures that were still in any sense alive.

~Elias Canetti[14]

This is an area into which few media critics have delved: a thorough content analysis of the major news outlets on the web. One of the reasons web content isn't adequately examined is that so much of it no longer exists. Due to the ephemeral nature of the medium, web content often disappears into a black hole. For example, I could easily look at a ten-year period in the history of newspapers (catalogued and stored in libraries, they become part of the historical record) and assess the content. But if I wanted to pull together a book of Internet news blunders, and I wanted to include that "NATO Plane Downed" headline, it would be impossible. There's little chance that Fox still has digital or hard copy. At Fox, I was told, 'Get the story up fast. If it's wrong, pull it off the server and destroy it. No one will ever know the difference.' I can't even find a single article I wrote during my Fox tenure. And unless libraries get in the business of documenting every version of every story ever posted on every major Internet news site, we won't have any 'Dewey Wins' headlines in the future—a huge blow for scholarship.

~Tatiana Siegel[15]

Chapter Ten: Guardians of History

Unlike print, electronic data accords its producer the means to retain and protect exclusive ownership rights. No longer are publishers confined to packaging data and selling it outright to libraries and other customers to use in perpetuity. They can treat electronic information like rental property, subdividing and leasing it to their customers on terms carefully delimited by contract ...

In an era when government vacillates in meeting its obligation to secure the public's information rights, libraries may be the only civic agency positioned to defend the community's stake in equal access. If we accept this essentially democratic trust, it follows that our role is to bridge, rather than widen, economic gaps in the information chain, thereby reasserting the social and political value of information that some would renounce.

~John Haar[16]

Chapter Eleven: Social Responsibility

The real weakness in the social responsibility movement is not that ALA will impose a position upon librarians but that librarians will fail to impose a position upon the ALA.

~Robert Wedgeworth[1]

Chapter Eleven: Social Responsibility

The demand for 'relevance' by the Social Responsibilities Round Table, and related movements in the ALA, can be traced back to the nineteenth-century faith in the public library as a social force that would, through the promotion of reading, save mankind from poverty, crime, vice, alcoholism, and almost every other evil to which flesh is heir. But a more striking parallel to the present day unrest is to be found in the pleas of the young librarians for social action during the 1930s, for ferment was also taking place in the profession during that decade. The storms of crisis that battered the American economy during the last years of the Hoover Administration and the first years of Roosevelt's promoted an awareness that the library had sociological roots, and that the librarian should have a vigorous and vocal social consciousness.

~Jesse Shera[2]

When the library profession becomes thoroughly conscious of precisely what it is trying to do and why it is doing it, we may hope to see a very significant change affecting not only libraries and librarians but also the society in which they serve. The bewildered groping which characterizes so much of our activity is largely the result of lack of a definite conception of our purposes.

~J. Periam Danton[3]

Accountability as a trend for public institutions (public schools are the earliest example) was a self-imposed response to conservative questions concerning the value (in both the economic and qualitative meanings of that term) received for the tax dollars spent. The idea has since become much more crudely economic in the intervening years, with direct threats to cut or withhold funding or privatize all or part of public institutions that are not "performing." In turn, accountability has given rise to research on qualitative measures as a means to justify budgets or encourage private donations. This reorientation of the profession represents a philosophical change in outlook, as John Budd argues. When talked about and written about this way, the presupposition is that libraries provide collections and services (and "account" for and evaluate them) not as an end but in exchange or as a means, and the 'desired end is really the material success of the library.' Such practices are not harmless, trendy adaptations to altered circumstances, but a reorientation of librarianship along the lines of the new public philosophy, with significant contradictions to the public sphere role of libraries ...

~John Buschman[4]

ALA recognizes its broad social responsibilities. The broad social responsibilities of the American Library Association are defined in terms of the contribution that librarianship can make in ameliorating or solving the critical problems of society; support for efforts to help inform and educate the people of the United States on these problems and to encourage them to examine the many views on and the facts regarding each problem; and the willingness of ALA to take a position on current critical issues with the relationship to libraries and library service set forth in the position statement.

~ALA Policy Manual, article 1.1[5]

Libraries should permit and encourage a full and free expression of views by staff on professional and policy matters.

~Sandy Berman's suggested addition to the Library Bill of Rights[6]

The quality of belligerency was never more greatly needed in the profession than it is at this moment. We have been called many things in our time—gentle and genteel; modest and mousy; learned and lame; dedicated and dowdy; unprepossessing and underpaid. I hope for the day when we shall be called the belligerent profession. ... I would have us be belligerent first within the ranks of our profession. We have never, in my opinion, stood our ground firmly enough and declared what our peculiar, unique function was to be, and then held to it and accomplished it.

~Frances Clarke Sayers[7]

The two professions most often identified as the models toward which all others strive are medicine and law. The goal of medicine is healing. Regardless of new pharmaceuticals or improved diagnostics, the goal is healing. The goal of law is justice. Regardless of computerized case searching or scientific forensics, the goal is justice. Librarianship, thanks to centuries of effort, has a simple and clear goal as well. Applying Ockham's Razor, that entities are not to be multiplied beyond necessity, the goal is information equity. Inherent in this goal is working for universal literacy; defending intellectual freedom; preserving and making accessible the human record; and ensuring that preschoolers have books to read.

~Kathleen de la Peña McCook[8]

I consider it important, indeed urgently necessary, for intellectual workers to get together, both to protect their own economic status and, also, generally speaking, to secure their influence in the political field.

~Albert Einstein[9]

The Way of the Library is like the bending of the bow.
The high is lowered and the low is raised.
If the string is too long, it is shortened;
if there is not enough, it is made longer.
The Way of the Library is to take from those who have enough for the benefit of the entire community.

~From *The Librarian's Lau Tzu: The Book of the Library and Its Ways*[10]

We have a situation, therefore, where, in general terms, one third of the population is middle class and yet this class makes up two thirds of library users; conversely, two thirds of the population are working class, but this class makes up only one third of library users.

~John Pateman[11]

Does the black militant, political rebel, Chicano, or Establishment-shy youth find what he wants in the neighborhood or college library? No, baby. And it doesn't require a year-long, carefully-conducted, foundation-funded study to prove it. Everybody knows it.

The point is this: No amount of talk at library conferences and round tables about "relevancy" and "social responsibility" is itself going to enliven, enrich, un-barnacle, and, yes, controversialize library collections. Only librarians themselves can actually make their wares relevant to the whole community they serve: not just the respectable, well-shaven, white middle class (who, in any event, ought to know what's going on elsewhere from more trustworthy sources than Time/Life), but also the dissidents, the increasingly self-aware minorities, the forces in motion.

If this appears to suggest that most libraries are insufferably "square," that the profession is murdering its own noble "Bill of Rights" by ignoring it, and that literally millions of deprived, oppressed, and disaffected, yet wonderfully creative, sensitive, and energetic people simply don't find much nourishment or stimulation in the library—well, that's right.

~Sandy Berman[12]

Chapter Twelve: Neutrality

Silence is the language of complicity.

~Unknown

Chapter Twelve: Neutrality

Many librarians hold the reassuring belief that all information is neutral and therefore the library's collection development decisions do not involve judgments about whether some information is good or bad. But for many librarians and community activists this is not the case. The belief that some information is morally wrong and that the use of these resources can lead to moral decay reflects the same concern of early library leaders.

~Mark Alfino and Linda Pierce[1]

No fair historical examination of librarianship in America could fail to note ... that its annals are replete with examples of partisanship, albeit not necessarily (as one would like to believe) of free thought or the rights of minorities, but too often of the causes of the powers-that-be and the forces of order, sometimes taking the form of a passive defense of the status quo, sometimes taking shape as an active campaign for a new cause.

~Mark Rosenzweig[2]

To ensure a comprehensive and non-sectarian collection of material on all subjects requires a social project of great complexity. Yet as people charged with providing public access to knowledge easily equal to that of the academic, the doctor or the politician. They have the task of providing a democratic society with the information to preserve, even to improve that democracy. They are required to be unbiased and to serve everyone equally. Censorship promotes elitism, the enemy of democracy. Selection should act as a leveler. It should not ignore marginal interests. If they are to work effectively as agents for social and cultural education librarians need to engage in an activism that is largely lacking in the profession.

~Chris Atton[3]

If you believe, as I do, that the difference between *The Nation* and *The National Review* and *The New York Times*, in terms of ideology, is that *The Nation* has the ideology of the liberal left, and the *National Review* has the ideology of the conservative right, I would say *The New York Times Magazine*—and the mainstream media writ large—has the ideology of the center, and it is part of the ideology of the center to deny that it has an ideology.

~Victor Navasky[4]

Chapter Twelve: Neutrality

There are those who, clinging to the idea that the library profession should be politically neutral, would contend that contributing to social projects is not an appropriate activity for librarians. However, without a clear and vital set of philosophical and political ideals acting as a guiding beacon, the library profession will not remain neutral, but will drift aimlessly with the currents of power and privilege.

Librarians must forcefully articulate their commitment to serving the information needs of all segments of society. They must rededicate themselves to assuring the widest and most equitable access to information by opposing fees for services and the commercialization of knowledge. Furthermore, librarians must be willing to enter the political arena and advocate for these principles.

~Henry Blanke[5]

If information is not neutral, if moral judgments are part of information usage, and if one of our jobs as a profession is to recognize those judgments and to make decisions, it would seem that certain principles of truth, justice, equality, and freedom must be defining values of the profession.

~Mark Alfino & Linda Pierce[6]

There are all sorts of ways that library materials might be balanced upon the basis of opposing interests, values, and opinions. Furthermore, the idea of balance has numerous relations.

There is, for example, the dictum that the collection should represent All Points of View. Since every book expresses a view distinct from that of every other, the addition of any book to the collection disturbs that "balance," however slightly.

Special pleading for O.K. values is also closely related to the notion of balance. That a book is "for" or "against" Patriotism, Morality, or Religion—or for that matter, Freedom, Democracy, or Civil Rights—hardly seems sufficient reason for either its automatic selection or rejection. "For America First" and "We shall overcome" may be seen as admirable sentiments or not, depending on one's point of view, but they are not principles of book selection.

Neither, to be sure, is Public Demand. When a librarian says of a good book, "It will be a shelf-sitter," this may not only be a bad guess and a weak excuse for rejecting it; it is often also a presumptuous downgrading of the public's intelligence, which must be assumed to be at least as considerable as our own.

~Ronald Landor[7]

Chapter Twelve: Neutrality

> The library is not an institution which exists removed from our increasingly interdependent and politicized world. The professionals who control America's information institutions ... cannot retreat into those institutions and ignore the larger society. The result of this sort of myopic professionalism is to support intellectual freedom for those who have power while denying it to those who are powerless.
>
> ~Jane Robbins[8]

> We librarians ostensibly subscribe to the "balanced collection" professional ethic. Intellectual freedom, our *raison d'être*, needs a garden of diversity in which to flourish. So we can certainly demand equal time for women's material after 5,000 years of male worldview! I define "women's material" as material useful to women, which works directly in our interest like a fine tool, which does not ignore, trivialize, or lie to us.
>
> ~Celeste West[9]

Nothing contributes more to peace of soul than having no opinion at all.

~Georg Christoph Lichtenberg[10]

The most unpardonable sin in society is independence of thought.

~Emma Goldman[11]

We shall succeed only so far as we continue that most distasteful of all activity, the intolerable labor of thought.

~Judge Learned Hand[12]

Washing one's hands of the conflict between the powerful and the powerless means to side with the powerful, not to be neutral.

~Paulo Freire[13]

The death of democracy is not likely to be an assassination from ambush. It will be a slow extinction from apathy, indifference, and undernourishment.

~Robert Maynard Hutchins[14]

Chapter Thirteen: Liberty or Slavery

A library is an arsenal of liberty.

~Unknown

Chapter Thirteen: Liberty or Slavery

Never regard your study as a duty, but as the enviable opportunity to learn to know the liberating influence of beauty in the realm of spirit for your own personal joy and to the profit of the community to which your later work belongs.

~Albert Einstein, in a message to a Princeton freshman publication, *The Dink*[1]

Frederick Douglas taught that literacy is the path from slavery to freedom. There are many kinds of slavery and many kinds of freedom. But reading is still the path.

~Carl Sagan[2]

To be literate is to possess the cow of plenty.
~Madras Library Association[3]

Thought is subversive and revolutionary, destructive and terrible, Thought is merciless to privilege, established institutions, and comfortable habit. Thought is great and swift and free.

~Bertrand Russell[4]

To make a contented slave it is necessary to make a thoughtless one. It is necessary to darken his moral and mental vision, and, as far as possible, to annihilate the power of reason.

~Frederick Douglas[5]

Education for freedom must begin by stating facts and enunciating values, and must go on to develop appropriate techniques for realizing the values and for combating those who, for whatever reason, choose to ignore the facts or deny the values.

~Aldous Huxley[6]

Only the educated are free.
~Epictetus[7]

Loyalty to a petrified opinion never yet broke a chain or freed a human soul.

~Mark Twain[8]

Be not a slave of words.
~Thomas Carlyle[9]

They that can give up essential liberty to obtain a little temporary safety deserve neither liberty nor safety.

~Benjamin Franklin[10]

A people that wants to be free must arm itself with a free press.

~George Seldes[11]

Chapter Fourteen: Truth & Lie

The very concept of objective truth is fading out of the world. Lies will pass into history.

~George Orwell[1]

Chapter Fourteen: Truth & Lie

Truth is a good dog; but beware of barking too close to the heels of error, lest you get your brains kicked out.

~Samuel Taylor Coleridge[2]

Truth often suffers more by the heat of its defenders than the arguments of its opposers.

~William Penn[3]

Bolshevism is knocking at our gates, we can't afford to let it in. ... We must keep America whole and safe and unspoiled. We must keep the worker away from red literature and red ruses; we must see that his mind remains healthy.

~Al Capone[4]

You may not be able to change the world, but at least you can embarrass the guilty.

~Jessica Mitford[5]

To tell the truth is revolutionary.
~Antonio Gramsci[6]

The first casualty of war is truth.
~Aeschylus[7]

We had both agreed that my reflections would have more force if I were to describe these circles of corruption in a flat, straightforward style, rather like that of a cookbook. I think, immodestly perhaps, that the result is quite interesting; certainly, it is unlike the evangelical style of most American journalists, who proclaim their partisanship in such a shrill way that even when they are telling the truth they sound false or, worse, paid for.

~Charlie Schermerhorn Schuyler, in Gore Vidal's historical novel, *1876*[8]

The real advantage which truth has, consists in this, that when an opinion is true, it may be extinguished once, twice, or many times, but in the course of ages there will generally be found persons to rediscover it, until some one of its reappearances falls on a time when from favorable circumstances it escapes persecution until it has made such head as to withstand all subsequent attempts to suppress it.

~John Stuart Mill[9]

> Every journalist owes tribute to the evil one.
>
> ~Henri de la Fontaine[10]

I am a firm believer in the people. If given the truth, they can be depended upon to meet any national crisis. The great point is to bring them the real facts.

~Abraham Lincoln[11]

A man that should call everything by its right name would hardly pass the street without being knocked down as a common enemy.

~George Savile, First Marquess of Halifax[12]

Let not men think there is no truth but in the sciences that they study, or books that they read. To prejudge other men's notions before we have looked into them is not to show their darkness but to put out our own eyes.

~John Locke[13]

> From error to error one discovers the entire truth.
>
> ~Sigmund Freud[14]

Chapter Fifteen: Secrecy

A little sunlight is the best disinfectant.

~U.S. Supreme Court Justice Louis Brandeis[1]

Chapter Fifteen: Secrecy

The liberties of a people never were, nor ever will be, secure, when the transactions of their rulers may be concealed from them.

~Patrick Henry[2]

A popular government, without popular information, or the means of acquiring it, is but a prologue to a farce or a tragedy; or, perhaps both.

~James Madison[3]

I believe that a guarantee of public access to government information is indispensable in the long run for any democratic society. ... If officials make public only what they want citizens to know, then publicity becomes a sham and accountability meaningless.

~Sissela Bok[4]

Documentation is like sex: when it is good, it is very, very good; and when it is bad, it is still better than nothing.

~Dick Brandon[5]

If there be time to expose through discussion the falsehood and the fallacies, to avert the evil by the processes of education, the remedy to be applied is more speech, not enforced silence.

~Louis Dembitz Brandeis[6]

Better to light a candle than to curse the darkness.

~Chinese proverb

How often, or on what system, the Thought Police plugged in on any individual wire was guesswork. It was even conceivable that they watched everybody all the time. But at any rate they could plug in your wire whenever they wanted to. You had to live—did live, from habit that became instinct—in the assumption that every sound you made was overheard, and, except in darkness, every movement scrutinized.

~George Orwell, in *1984*[7]

Notes

Chapter One: On Books and Reading

1. This proverb is found in some sources that attribute it as a Chinese Proverb. See Connie Robertson, ed. *The Wordsworth Dictionary of Quotations* (Wordsworth, 1998) 339; other sources attribute it as Arabian. See Lilless McPherson Shilling and Linda K. Fuller, eds. *Dictionary of Quotations in Communications* (Greenwood, 1997) 27; still, other sources attribute the proverb as American. See Elizabeth Knowles, ed. *The Oxford dictionary of phrase, saying, and quotation* (Oxford, 1997) 48.

2. Ralph Waldo Emerson (1803–1882), American philosher, essayist and poet, in his personal journal, 7 June 1841; found in *Journals of Ralph Waldo Emerson* (Houghton Mifflin, 1911) 561.

3. Johann Wolfgang von Goethe (1749–1832), German writer; quoted by Edward C. Goodman and Ted Goodman, eds. *Forbe's Book of Business Quotations* (Workman, 2008) 75.

4. Voltaire (1694–1778), French writer and philosher, in *A Philosophical Dictionary* (1764); found in 1843 reprint *A Philosophical Dictionary, Vol.2* (Dugdale) 164.

5. Joseph Brodsky (b.1940), Russian-born U.S. poet, in his 1987 Nobel Prize acceptance speech; quoted by Robert Andrews, *The Columbia Dicionary of Quotations* (Columbia, 1993) 20.

6. (Doubleday, 1999).

7. Jim Trelease (b.1941), American educator and author, quoted by Linton Weeks in "Aliteracy: Read All About It, or Maybe Not; Millions of Americans Who Can Read Choose Not To. Can We Do Without the Written Word?," *Washington Post* 14 May 2001: C01. The Web edition was titled: "The No-Book Report: Skim It and Weep; Millions of Americans Who Can Read Choose Not To. Can We Do Without the Written Word?".

8. Quoted by John Berry in "I'm Proud To Be a Librarian," his May 1998 *Library Journal* editorial. It was misattributed in the original *Library Juice Quote of the Week* to the late Arthur Curley, ALA president from 1994–95; After reading the editorial, I discovered that it was not Curley who posed this question to Berry, but rather an anonymous "debating adversary". See John Berry, "I'm proud to be a librarian," *Library Journal* 1 May 1998: 6.

9. This has been attributed in various places as the WWII slogan of the American Library Association, The Council of Books in Wartime, and the US Office of War Information. The correct source is The Council of Books in Wartime, of which many American Library Association members were members of. Both ALA and the US Office of War Information appropriated the slogan for their publications of the time, but the slogan gained most of it's notoriety from propaganda posters distributed by the US Office of War Information.

10. Ezra Pound (1885–1972), American expatriate poet, critic and intellectual; quoted by Robertson 336.

11. Salman Rushdie (b.1947), Indian-British novelist and essayist, in "The Power of the Pen: Does Writing Change Anything?", his address to the PEN American Center's World Voices Conference, 18 April 2005. This excerpt was quoted in the 23 April 2005 *The Guardian UK* book review section, and the entire speech was published as an opinion piece in the 24 April 2005 *Los Angeles Times Online*.

12. Henry David Thoreau (1817–1862), American author and philosopher, in *Walden, or, Life in the Woods* (Houghton Mifflin: 1910) 120.

13. Malcolm X (Malcolm Little, 1925–1965), American civil rights leader, in *The Autobiography of Malcolm X* published posthumously in 1966. Found in Malcolm X, et.al., The Autobiography of Malcolm X (Ballantine, 1973) 182.

14. Fidel Castro (b.1926), Cuban revolutionary leader; quoted by Mario Mencia, *The Fertile Prison: Fidel Castro in Batista's Jails* (Ocean, 1993) 36.

15. Mike Tyson (b.1966), American boxer, quoted by Tom FitzGerald, "Tyson No Longer Has Time for the Classics," *San Francisco Chronicle* 6 Sept. 1996: D6.

16. G.M. Trevelyan (1876–1962), English historian, in *English Social History* (Longman's, 1942) 582.

17. Doris Lessing (b.1919), British writer and winner of the Nobel Prize for Literature in 2007, in the introduction to her book *The Golden Notebook* (Harper Collins, 1999) xii–xxiv.

18. Sir William Osler (1849–1919), Canadian physician, in "Books and Men," *Aequanimitas* (P. Blakiston's Son & Co., 1906) 221.

19. Henri Michaux (1899–1984), Belgian poet and writer, in *Porteaux d'Angle*. Found in the English translation by Lynn Hogard, *Tent Posts* (Green Integer, 1997) 155.

20. Woody Allen (b.1935), American film director and playwright, in interview with Richard J.H. Johnston, "You Name It, Woody Is Doing It," *New York Times* 14 Feb. 1969: 26.

21. David Foster Wallace (b.1962), American writer; (Little, Brown and Co., 1996) 12.

22. Lucius Annaeus Seneca (4 BC–65 AD), Spanish born Roman statesman, philosopher and moralist, in *Epistolae Morale*; quoted by Vladimir Wertsman, *The Librarian's Companion* (Greenwood, 1996) 144.

23. Garrison Keillor (b.1942), U.S. writer and broadcaster, in "epigraph," *The Book of Guys* (Viking, 1993).

Chapter Two: On Libraries

1. Jorge Luis Borges (1899–1986), Argentine writer. Found in Shilling and Fuller 135. This quotation has also been attributed to John Cheever; see Richard Lederer, *The Miracle of Language* (Simon and Schuster, 1999) 156.

2. Martin Luther King Jr. (1929–1968), American civil rights leader, printed in the program at ALA midwinter 2000, "Celebrating Equity and Empowerment," on Martin Luther King Day.

3. From a conversation with Rory Litwin.

4. Marie de Sevigne (1626–1696), French diarist, in *Letters of Madame de Sevigne to Her Daughter and Friends* (Roberts Brothers, 1878) 225.

5. Elie Wiesel (b.1928), Jewish writer, activist and Nobel Laureate, in *From the Kingdom of Memory: Reminiscences* (Summit, 1990) 48.

6. Saul Bellow (1915–2005), Canadian-American writer; Found in Shilling and Fuller 135.

7. Jane Langton (b.1922), American mystery writer and author of children's literature, in *The Thief of Venice: A Homer Kelly Mystery* (Viking, 1999) 38.

8. 3 March 2002, 1 Sept. 2008 <http://www.metafilter.com/16878/>; emphasis from original.

9. Joan Bauer (b.1951), American author of young adult literature; (Putnam, 1997) 142.

10. Norman Mailer (1923–2007), American writer and journalist, in "A librarian interviews with Norman Mailer" *American Libraries* July/August 1980: 411–412.

11. Germaine Greer (b.1939) Australian-born Eglish literature critic and noted feminist, in "Still in Melbourne, January 1987," *Daddy, We Hardly Knew You* (1989). Found in Andrews 519.

12. Samuel Johnson (1709–1784), Engish essayist, poet and biographer, in *The Rambler* March 23, 1751; Found in *The Rambler. In Three Volumes* Vol. II, 16th ed. (Luke Hansard & Sons, 1810) 222.

13. Jennifer Vogel, author and columnist for Minneapolis culture rag *The Rake*, in "Can the Public Library (and Democracy) Survive?," *The Rake*, Feb. 2005, 1 Sept. 2008 <http://www.rakemag.com/reporting/features/can-public-library-and-democracy-survive>.

14. Doris Lessing (b.1919), British writer and winner of the Nobel Prize for Literature in 2007; quoted by Karen Weekes, *Women Know Everything!: 3,241 Quips, Quotes, & Brilliant Remarks* (Quirk, 2007) 350.

15. Andrew Carnegie (1835–1919), Scottish American industrialist and philanthropist; quoted by Bill Bradfield, ed. *Books and Reading: A Book of Quotations* (Dover, 2002) 12.

16. Thomas Carlyle (1795–1881), Scottish essayist, satirist, and historian, and founder of the London Library, in his personal journal, May 18, 1832; quoted by Thomas Kelly, *History of Public Libraries in Great Britain 1845–1965* (London Library Association, 1973) 6.

17. I, ii, 109–110.

18. Jesse Shera (1903–1982), American librarian and information scientist, in *The Foundations of Education for Librarianship* (John Wiley and Sons, 1972) 108.

19. Maurice J. (Mitch) Freedman (b.1940), ALA Councilor and past-president, in an Interview with *Library Juice*, 7 March 2001, 1 Sept. 2008 <http://www.libr.org/juice/issues/vol4/LJ_4.8.sup.html>.

20. Quoted in the ALA national campaign "Libraries Change Lives," and later in Michael Gorman's *Our Singular Strengths: Meditations for Librarians* (ALA, 1998) 96.

21. Ann Herbert (b.1952), American writer and past editor of the now ceased *CoEvolution Quarterly*; quoted by Fred R. Shapiro and Joseph Epstein, eds. *Yale Book of Quotations* (2006) 356. This quote is a modification of "Dope will get you through times of no money better than money will get you through times of no dope. From *Freewheelin' Franklin of the Fabulous Furry Freak Brothers*, an underground comic by Gilbert Shelton.

22. Walter Cronkite (b.1916), American broadcast journalist and anchorman. Found in *Documents to the People* Sept. 1994: 169 (sidebar).

23. Malcolm X, et.al. 183. (See Note 13, Chapter One for details.)

24. Lily Tomlin (b.1939), American comedian and actress, found on her official website. She actually attributes this and many of her famous quips to her writer, Jane Wagner.

25. Season 1, episode 10, 21 Dec. 1969.

Chapter Three: Information Technology

1. David Temkin, American Web engineer and technology blogger, subtitle of his ceased magazine, *In Formation*, and blog, 2 Feb. 2007, 1 Sept. 2008 <http://www.davidtemkin.com/>.

2. Eli M. Noam (b.1946), professor of Finance and Economics, in "Electronics and the Dim Future of the University," *Science* 13 Oct. 1995: 249.

Notes

3. Hakim Bey (Peter Lamborn Wilson, b.1945), American political writer, essayist, and poet, in *The Lemonade Ocean and Modern Times—A Position Paper by Hakim Bey*, 7 April 1991, 1 Sept. 2008 <http://www.hermetic.com/bey/lemonade.html>.

4. Bernard Vavrek, American library science professor, in "Your Public Library Has a Web Page: So What?," *American Libraries* Jan. 1999: 50.

5. Joseph Weizenbaum (1923–2008), German-American author and professor of computer science, in *Computer Power and Human Reason: From Judgment to Calculation* (W. H. Freeman, 1976) 203.

6. Sanford (Sandy) Berman (b.1933), American activist librarian and cataloger, in "'Inside' Censorship" a talk given at a Minnesota Atheists meeting, 18 November 2000; later published in *Progressive Librarian* Summer 2001: 53.

7. Neil Postman (1931–2003), American professor, media theorist, and cultural critic, in *Informing Ourselves to Death*, A speech given at a meeting of the German Informatics Society (Gesellschaft fuer Informatik), 11 Oct. 1990, 1 Sept. 2008, <http://www.archive.org/details/openmind_ep1095>.

8. "Librarianship and Information Science," *The Study of Information: Interdisciplinary Messages*, ed. Fritz Machlup and Una Mansfield (Wiley, 1983) 385.

9. Michael Joyce (b.1945), American author and professor of English, in *Othermindedness: The Emergence of Network Culture* (University of Michigan, 2000) 63.

10. Robert Hauptman (b.1941), professor of information media at St. Cloud State University and the editor of the *Journal of Information Ethics* in "Information Technology: Seduction and Peril" *Educom Review* May/June 1998: 48.

11. Phil Agre, American author and professor of information studies, in "The End of Information and the Future of Libraries," *Progressive Librarian*, Spring/Summer 1997: 6.

12. Sven Birkerts (b.1951), American essayist and literary critic, in *The Gutenberg Elegies* (Faber & Faber, 1994) 129.

13. *Amusing Ourselves to Death: Public Discourse in the Age of Show Business* (Penguin, 1985) 140.

14. UUNet's internal catch-phrase; found in: "Editorial: NGN—A Fancy Feast of Networking Ideas," *Business Communications Review* Dec. 1998: 6.

15. Walt Crawford, American librarian and writer and speaker on libraries, technology, policy and media, in *Being Analog: Creating Tomorrow's Libraries* (ALA, 1999) 5.

16. I was unable to find the primary source for this quotation. It is posted on possibly hundreds of websites, all of which attribute Ghandi, but none of which provide the source. According to Ralph Keyes' *The Quote Verifier* there is scant evidence that Gandhi ever said this; I include it here and attribute it to Gandhi because of it's pervasiveness and the lack of evidence to contradict its authenticity. See Ralph Keyes, *The Quote Verifier* (Macmillan, 2006) 76.

17. *Technopoly: The Surrender of Culture to Technology* (Vintage, 1993) 67.

Chapter Four: Information Control

1. At his valedictory dinner, ALA Annual 1999, New Orleans.

2. Herbert Schiller (1919–2000), American media critic, sociologist, author, and scholar, in *Information Inequality: The Deepening Social Crisis in America* (Routledge, 1996) 36.

3. Bill Katz (1924–2004), American reference librarian and author of library literature, in his foreword to Sanford Berman's *Worth Noting: Editorials, Letters, Essays, an Interview, and Bibliography* (McFarland, 1988) vii.

4. Interviewed by Jim Dwyer for *Technicalities* Oct. 1986: 9. Reprinted in Berman, *Worth Noting* 132.

5. In a statement to OCLC and Hennepin County Library (MN); the statement was sent to several email lists, and can be found in its entirety on *The Sanford Berman Website*, 2 March 1999, 1 Sept. 2008 <http://www.sanfordberman.org/hcl/appeal.htm>.

6. Peter McDonald, (b.1952), Progressive librarian and activist, in "Corporate inroads & librarianship: the fight for the soul of the new millenium" *Progressive Librarian* Spring/Summer, 1997: 42.

7. Zoia Horn (b.1918), American reference librarian, in *Zoia! Memoirs of Zoia Horn, Battler for the People's Right to Know* (McFarland, 1995) 200–201.

8. Melvil Dewey (1851–1931), American librarian, educator, and the inventor of the Dewey Decimal Classification system, in "The Relation of the State to the Public Library," reprinted from *Transactions and Proceedings fo the Second International Library Conference, 1889*, and published in Barbara McCrimmon, ed. *American Library Philosophy: An Anthology*, (Shoe String Press, 1975) 4.

9. Response to a librarians@tao.ca list member who was tired of hearing anarchist librarian jokes and wanted a pithy comeback; March 1999.

10. Carla Hayden, former ALA President, in Kerry Gillespie, "Forget the sensible shoes: Librarians turn a new leaf," *Toronto Star* 14 June 2003: A01.

11. In a talk on 'Bibliocide by Cataloging', October 26, 1999, which included many examples. Most of the subject headings Berman offered as needed for adoption by LC had a political aspect—to their exclusion as well as to their need—but are justifiable simply based on sound cataloging principles.

12. Lara Jennifer Moore, American librarian and author, in *Restoring Order: The Ecole des Chartes and the Organization of Archives and Libraries in France, 1820–1870* (Litwin Books, 2008) 208–209.

13. Sir William Berkeley (1605–1677), British Royal Governor of the Colony of Virginia, 1671. Found in Frederick Converse Beach and George Edwin Rines, eds. "Public, or Common, Schools," *The Encyclopedia Americana* 1904 ed.

14. Albert Einstein (1879–1955), German-American physicist, educator, celebrity, Nobel Prize winner and cultural icon, in his forward to Lincoln Kinnear Barnett's *The Universe and Dr. Einstein* (Sloane, 1950) 1.

15. Al Gore (b.1948), former U.S. Senator and Vice President of the United States, speaking at a conference at New School University on "The Uses and Misuses of Fear," quoted by Eric Alterman, "Al, We Hardly Know Ye," *The Nation* 1 March 2004: 12.

16. Andre Schiffrin (b.1935), American author, publisher, socialist and co-founder of Students for a Democratic Society, in *The Business of Books: How the International Conglomerates Took Over Publishing and Changed the Way We Read* (Verso, 2000) 103–4.

17. In the preface to their book *Manufacturing Consent* (Pantheon, 1988) xi.

18. Joseph Urgo, American professor of English, in In *The Age of Distraction* (University of Mississippi, 2000) 37.

19. Alex Carey, Australian sociologist and author; found in *Taking the Risk out of Democracy: Corporate Propaganda Versus Freedom and Liberty* ed. Andrew Lohrey (University of Illinois Press, 1997) 18.

20. In an editorial about how *Time Magazine* neglected to mention, in its bio on their Person of the Century, that Einstein was a socialist. See Thomas Gallagher, "In Fact …," *The Nation* 24 Jan. 2000: 7. The original (and full) quotation can be found in Einstein's collection of essays, *Out of My Later Years* (Citadel, 1995) 129.

21. Gore Vidal (b.1925), American novelist and critic, in *A View from the Diners Club: Essays 1987–1991* (Deutsch, 1991) 187.

22. Hermann Goering (1893–1946) Nazi Reichsmarschall and Adolf Hitler's #2 Man, from his Nuremberg jail cell while awaiting trial for war crimes. Found in G.M. Gilbert, *Nuremberg Diary* (Da Capo, 1995) 278.

23. Carey 21. (See Note 19 for details.)

24. Found in Howard Kurtz, "Journalists Worry About Limits on Information, Access," *Washington Post* 24 Sept. 2001: A05.

25. James Madison (1751–1836), American founding father and fourth president of the United States, in a letter to Thomas Jefferson dated 13 May 1798. Found in *Letters and Other Writings of James Madison* (Lippincott, 1865) 141.

26. Francis Bacon (1561–1626), English Philosopher; found in *Novum Organum* ed. Joseph Devey, M.A., (Collier & Son, 1902) 62.

27. William Kuhns (b.1943), American media, technology and religion scholar, in *The Information Explosion* (Thomas Nelson, 1971) 82.

28. Mark Weisbrot, co-director of the Center for Economic and Policy Research in Washington D.C., in "Are White House Scandals the Beginning of the End," *AlterNet*, 22 May 2002, 2 Sept. 2008 <http://www.alternet.org/columnists/story/13198/are_white_house_scandals_the_beginning_of_the_end/>.

29. Morris (Mo) Udall (1922–1998), former U.S. Representative from Arizona, in an interview with Tom Wicker, "The Fourth Law of Politics," *New York Times* 4 May 1975: 225.

30. Mark Twain (Samuel Langhorne Clemens 1835–1910), American author and satirist, quoted by *Reader's Digest Quotable Quotes* 194.

31. From an interview for the *Nieuwe Rotterdamsche Courant* 1921; restated in Einstein's memoirs, *Mein Weltbild* published in 1933. Found in *The World as I See It*, trans. Alan Harris (Citidel, 1979) 41.

32. Laura Moriarty, Deputy Director at Small Press Distribution in Berkeley, CA., in a conversation with Rory Litwin at their booth at ALA Midwinter, 2001.

33. I was unable to find the source of this widely quoted statement, though I suspect it is a paraphrase of a passage in Chomsky's postscript to *Turning the Tide: U.S. Intervention in Central America and the Struggle for Peace* (South End, 1985) 275. The original statement was in regard to U.S. support of the Contras in the 1980's: "The uniformity and obedience of the media, which any dictator would admire, thus succeeds in concealing what is plainly the real reason for the U.S. attack, sometimes conceded openly by Administration spokesmen."

34. Vigdor Schreibman (b.1928), journalist, publisher and constitutional scholar, in *Schreibman v. Holmes et al.* September 1997, in an unsuccessful attempt to keep alive his lawsuit to claim his right to be in the congressional press galleries as a journalist.

35. E. Persimmon, zine reviewer, in "I dream of a zine ...," *A reader's guide to the underground press* No. 12: 26.

36. Found in the introduction to Chris Dodge and Jan DeSirey, eds., *Everything You Always Wanted to Know About Sandy Berman but Were Afraid to Ask* (McFarland, 1995) x.

Chapter Five: Censorship

1. John Trenchard (1662–1723) and Thomas Gordon (1692–1750), in an essay published in the *London Journal* in 1722. The authors wrote colaboratively under the pen name Cato and their 144 essays published in the *London Journal* became known as *Cato's Letters*. This quotation is widely misattributed to Benjamin Franklin, who quoted a large tract from the *London Journal* peice, in a letter to the *The New-England Courant* 9 July 1722. Franklin also wrote using a pen name—Silence Dogwood—and he did not attribute the quoted tract in his letter.

2. Hubert H. Humphrey (1911–1978), thirty-eighth U.S. Vice President, serving under President Lyndon B. Johnson and former United States Senator from Minnesota, in response to having over 50 established authors and publishers walk out of his speech at the National Book Award Ceremonies in protest of the Vietnam War; found in Henry Raymont, "Writers Leave Humphrey Talk: 50 Join in Vietnam Protest at Book Awards," *New York Times* 9 March 1967: 42.

3. John F. Kennedy (1917–1963), Thirty-fifth U.S. President, in his *Voice of America* address, 26 Feb. 1962. "Kennedy Calls on 'Voice' to Tell Both Good and Bad About Nation: Heard Around World," *New York Times* 27 Feb. 1962: 17.

4. Michael Gorman (b.1941), British-American librarian and past president of ALA, in *The Value and Values of Libraries*, a talk given at the "Celebration of Libraries", Oxford, 20 September 2002.

5. Emma Goldman (1869–1940), Lithuanian-American women's rights activist and anarchist, quoted by Les Harding, *A Book in Hand Is Worth Two in the Library: Quotations on Books and Librarianship* (McFarland, 1994) 75.

6. Leon Carnovsky (1903–1975), American librarian and educator, in "The Obligations and Responsibilities of the Librarian Regarding Censorship," *Library Quarterly* Jan. 1950: 21.

7. Larry Flynt (b.1942), American pornographer and First Amendment activist; found in *Sex, Lies, & Politics* (Kensington, 2006) 21.

8. Oscar Wilde (1854–1900), Irish playwright, novelist, poet and author; (Random House, 1982) 205.

9. Henry Louis Gates, Jr. (b.1950), American literary critic, educator, scholar, writer, editor and public intellectual, in "2 Live Crew, Decoded," *New York Times* 19 June 1990: A23.

10. Dr. Laurence J. Peter (1919–1990), Candadian educator best known for his formulation of the *Peter Priciple*; quoted by Harding, 71.

11. Jeremy Bentham (1748–1832), English philosopher, in *Theory of Legislation*, trans. Richard Hildreth (K. Paul, Trench, Trübner & Co., 1908) 370–371.

12. Jason Blair, "Some Comic Strips Take an Unpopular Look at U.S.," *New York Times* 22 Oct. 2001: C9.

13. *In Good Faith* (Granta, 1990) 6.

14. Charles Willett, editor of *Counterpoise* and *Librarians at Liberty*, and former publisher of *Alternative Publishers of Books in North America*. Also former chair of the Alternatives In Print Task Force of ALA's Social Responsibilities Round Table; The quote is from a button that he created.

15. Carl Sagan (1934–1996), American astronomer, in "The Public Enemy," *Billions and Billions. Thoughts of Life and Death at the Brink of the Millennium*. (Ballantines, 1998) 189.

16. This is actually a paraphrase of *Martin v. Struthers*, 319 U.S. 141 (1943). This case was used as prior case law in the verdict of *Griswold v. Connecticut*, where the paraphrase can be found verbatim. I think the phrase more appropriately should be attributed to *Martin v. Struthers*, but since it is a paraphrase and not a direct quote, I left it as originally attributed in *Library Juice Quote of the Week*.

17. Alexander Berkman (1870–1936), American author and anarchist, found in Gene Fellner and Howard Zinn, *Life of an Anarchist: The Alexander Berkman Reader* (Seven Stories, 2004) xiv.

18. John Stuart Mill (1806–1873), British philosopher and economist, in *On Liberty* (Longmans, Green, and Co., 1913) 10.

19. According to Marc Rotenberg of the Electronic Privacy Information Center, XStop would filter out the U.S. Bill of Rights from Internet search results and block sites containing it, based upon its filtering algorithm

20. Melora Ranney Norman, American librarian, activist, and educator.

21. After testifying at a Sacramento, CA Library Commission Meeting on the new filtering system planned for the Sacramento Public Library; August 2001.

Chapter Six: Copyright

1. Kathy Ishizuka, "What's Mickey Afraid of?," *School Library Journal* Aug. 2002: 22. To see the offending rodent, see: <http://www.thegdl.org/kids/index.htm>.

2. Roy Tennant, American librarian, author, and digital library pioneer, in "The Copyright War," *Library Joural* 15 June 2001: 28.

3. Siva Vaidhyanathan (b.1966), American cultural historian and media scholar, in his talk at the 2005 ALA Annual Conference, "The Googlization of Everything: A Threat to the Information Commons?"

4. David Bollier, American public-interest policy strategist, journalist, activist and consultant, in "Why We Must Talk about the Information Commons," *Law Library Journal* Spring 2004: 280.

5. Thomas Jefferson (1743–1826), American founding father and third president of the United States, in an 1813 letter to Isaac McPherson on issues confronting patent law, quoted in Steven Johnson, "Marketplace of Ideas or Tag Sale?," *The Nation* 17 Dec. 2001: 25.

Chapter Seven: Data, Information, Knowledge & Other Wisdom

1. Margaret Atwood (b.1939), Canadian poet, novelist, and literary critic, in "Spelling," *True Stories* (Simon and Schuster, 1981) 64.

2. Machlup 384. (See Note 8, Chapter Three for details.)

3. *Amusing Ourselves to Death* 139; paraphrasing David Riesman.

4. Jean Baudrillard (1929–2007), French philosopher and sociologist, in *Cool Memories*, trans. Chris Turner (Verso, 1990) 219.

5. Stephen L. Talbot, author and *Netfuture* editor, original source unknown, but verified by Talbot in correspondence with the editor of this book.

6. "Information Does Not Equal Knowledge: Theorizing the Political Economy of Virtuality" *Journal of Computer Mediated Communication* Dec. 1997, 22 Sept. 2008 <http://www3.interscience.wiley.com/journal/120837735/abstract>.

7. Chris Fujiwara, writer, film critic, journalist, editor, and translator, in "Disintermediated!," *Hermenaut*, 7 Sept. 1998, 4 sept. 2008 <http://www.hermenaut.com/a54.shtml>.

8. Heinz von Foerster (1911–2002), Austrian-American physicist and philosopher; quoted by Kathleen Woodward, ed. *The Myths of Information: Technology and Postindustrial Culture* (Routledge & Kegan Paul, 1980) 19.

9. *Cosmos* (Ballantine, 1985) 238.

10. *The Letters of Oscar Wilde*, ed. Rupert Hart-Davis (Harcourt, Brace & World, 1962) 869.

11. Kurt Vonnegut (1922–2007), American novelist and satirist; quoted by Richard Todd, "The Masks of Kurt Vonnegut Jr.," *New York Times Magazine* 24 Jan. 1971: 31.

12. James Billington, Librarian of Congress, quoted in Joel Achenbach, "The Too-Much-Information Age: Today's Data Glut Jams Libraries and Lives. But Is Anyone Getting Any Wiser?," *Washington Post* 12 March 1999: A01.

13. Francis Morrone, American historian of architecture and *New York Sun* columnist, in "New York's Library in Cyberspace," *The New Criterion* Jan 1997: 79.

14. 18 April 1775; as quoted by Andrew Keogh in his address to the American Library Association Annual Conference in Asheville, North Carolina, 1907.

15. "New roles for information professionals in the development of consensus," a paper delivered at the LIANZA 2000 (Library and Information Association of New Zealand) Conference. In *Proceedings of LIANZA 2000, Christchurch, 15–18 October 2000*.

16. Antonio Gramsci (1891–1937), Italian philosopher, writer, politician and political theorist; quoted by Maurice A. Finocchiaro, *Beyond Right and Left: Democratic Elitism in Mosca and Gramsci* (Yale, 1999) 254.

17. David Bennahum, et. al., "Principle 4," *Principles of Technorealism*, 12 March 1998, 8 Sept. 2008 <http://www.technorealism.org/>.

18. Margaret Fuller (1810–1850), American writer, editor, intellectual, and feminist; quoted by Weekes, 240.

19. Enron, *Annual Report 2000* (Enron: 2001) 53; see: <http://picker.uchicago.edu/Enron/EnronAnnualsReport2000.pdf>.

20. Castle Rock Entertainment 1998.

21. Georg Lichtenberg (1742–1799), German scientist and satirist; in *Lichtenberg: A Doctrine of Scattered Occasions*, ed. Joseph Peter Stern (Indiana University, 1959) 143.

22. Frank Zappa (1940–1993), American composer, electric guitarist and rock musician, in "Packard Goose," *Joe's Garage* 1979: side three.

Chapter Eight: Information Overload

1. Gertrude Stein (1874–1946), American novelist, playright, and essayist, found in "Reflection on the Atomic Bomb," *Writings, 1932–1946: Stanzas in Meditation, Lectures in America, The Geographical History of America, Ida, Brewsie and Willie, Other Works*, ed. Catharine R. Stimpson (Library of America, 1998) 823.

2. Urgo 35. (See Note 18, Chapter Four for details.)

3. Herbert Simon (1916–2001), American political scientist and psychologist, in "Designing Organizatoins for an Information-Rich World," *Computers, Communications, and the Public Interest*, ed. Martin Greenburger (Johns Hopkins, 1971) 40–41.

4. Steven Johnson (b.1968), American popular science author, concluding his article in *Slate Magazine* about Amazon.com's new full text search, offering an inadvertent but comprehensive critique of the information society; 24 Oct. 2003, 14 Sept. 2008 <http://slate.msn.com/id/2090298/>.

5. Ray Bradbury (b.1920), American literary, fantasy, horror, science fiction, and mystery writer; found in *The Times Book of Quotations* (Times Books, 2000) 93.

6. Todd Gitlin (b.1943), American media critic, author, and professor of journalism, in a March 18, 2002 talk at The Commonwealth Club of California; 14 Sept. 2008, Transcript and audio at: <http://www.commonwealthclub.org/archive/02/02-03gitlin-speech.html>.

Notes

7. Günther Grass (b.1927), German author and playwright, in his interview for *New Statesman & Society*, 22 June, 1990: 37.

8. Achenbach A01. (See Note 12, Chapter Seven for details.)

9. Jack Van Impe (b.1930), American televangelist, of Jack Van Impe Ministries, in his late Sunday night television broadcast, 12 Nov. 2000.

Chapter Nine: On Librarians

1. Timothy Healy (1923–1992), Jesuit priest and former president of New York Public Library; quoted by Mitch Freedman in his draft mission statement for the Better Salaries/Pay Equity Task Force of the American Library Association Allied Professional Association, (date unkown), 14 Sept. 2008 <http://www.mjfreedman.org/tfmission.pdf>.

2. Catherine Drinker Bowen (1897–1973), American biographer, in *Adventures of a Biographer* (Little, Brown and Company, 195) 138–139.

3. "Cowboy Librarians," 13 Dec. 1997.

4. Elizabeth Martinez, former ALA Executive Director, in "The Education of Librarians: What is ALA's Role?," *American Libraries* Jan. 1997: 28. Also part of her San José State University SLIS graduation address, May, 1998.

5. James Danky (b.1947), American librarian and educator, in "Libraries: They Would Have Been a Good Idea," a talk given April 17, 1997 at the University of Illinois, Urbana-Champaign, and published in Sanford Berman and James Danky, eds., *Alternative Library Literature 1996–97* (McFarland, 1998) 4.

6. Machlup 385. (See Note 8, Chapter Three for details.)

7. Remarks on how librarians pressured Harper-Collins into reversing its decision to censor his new book; *Buzzflash* 12 March 2002, 16 Sept. 2008 <http://www.buzzflash.com/interviews/2002/03/Michael_Moore_031302.html>.

8. Louis Stanley Jast (1868–1944), British librarian, in his address to the 1904 General Meeting of the American Library Association; in *Papers and Proceedings of the Twenty-Sixth General Meeting of the American Library Association, St. Louis Mo. October 17–22, 1904* (American Library Association, 1904) 193.

9. Regis Philbin (b.1931), American television personality and gameshow host, in *Who Wants to Be a Millionaire?* 17 Feb. 2000.

10. Shera 202–3. (See Note 18, Chapter Two for details.)

11. Antonio Magliabecchi (1633–1714), librarian to Cosimo III, Grand Duke of Tuscany, in response to an insult from his enemies, the local Jesuits; quoted by Theodore Koch, *Some Old-Time Old-World Librarians* (The North American review publishing co., 1914) 3.

12. José Ortega y Gasset (1883–1955), Spanish philosopher and author; found in Wertsman, 142.

13. Derek Maraszek, age 13, in "School librarians valuable resource," *Santa Barbara News-Press* 25 June 2001: B1.

14. Patricia Glass Schuman, past-president of the American Library Association and cofounder of the Social Responsibilities Round Table, quoted by Leslie M. Campbell, "Keeping Watch on the Waterfront: Social Responsibility in Legal and Library Professional Organizations," *Law Library Journal* Summer 2000: 280; transcript of Shuman's speech given at the 1997 Annual Meeting of the American Association of Law Libraries.

15. Madonna (b.1958), American pop singer, songwriter, and actress, quoted by Jim Farber, "Melow Madonna," *New York Daily News* 27 Feb. 2000: 2.

16. troutfishing (Bruce Wilson), in his response to a *Metafilter* discussion regarding the subpoena of university records pertaining to anti-war activists, including librarian Christine Gaunt, who was charged with assaulting an officer when she went limp while being arrested. The subpoenas have since been dropped; 7 Feb. 2004, 16 Sept. 2008 <http://www.metafilter.com/mefi/31204>.

17. David Grenier, anarchist blogger, annotating his blog link to *Librarians Against War* Nov. 2001. This post no longer available at time of publishing.

18. "Gingerbread" season 3, episode 11, 12 Jan. 1999.

19. Derek de Solla Price (1922–1983), British historian of science, information scientist, and the father or Scientometrics, from the title of his paper presented at the 1979 Clinic on Library Applications of Data Processing, April 22–25 1979; found in *The Role of the Library in an Electronic Society* ed. Frederick W. Lancaster (University of Illinois, 1980) 8.

Chapter Ten: Guardians of History

1. Milan Kundera (b.1929), Czech born French author; trans. Michael Henry Heim (Knopf, 1980) 3.

2. George Orwell (Eric Arthur, 1903–1950), English writer, in "Freedom of the Park," *The Collected Essays, Journalism and Letters of George Orwell: Volume IV: In Front of Your Nose 1945–1959* eds. Sonia Orwell and Ian Angus (Harcourt, Brace & World, 1968) 40.

3. Michael Moore (b.1954), American filmmaker, author and actor, in "Muzzling Moore," *Salon* 7 Jan. 2002, 3 Sept. 2008 <http://dir.salon.com/story/books/feature/2002/01/07/moore/index.html>. Library Juice is mentioned a couple of times in this article.

4. Albert Einstein, in a letter to the National Emergency Civil Liberties Committee, March 3, 1954

5. Gary Klein, librarian and activist, marching with ALA members at the 1990 Chicago gay pride parade.

6. Schiller 35. (See Note 2, Chapter Four for details.)

7. Archie L. Dick, South African librarian, in "Epistemological Positions in Library and Information Science," *Library Quarterly* July 1999: 311.

8. "Legislators Save Washington State Library," *Information Today* 25 March 2002, 16 Sept. 2008 <http://newsbreaks.infotoday.com/wndReader.asp?ArticleId=17220>.

9. Louise S. Robbins, from the introduction to her book, *Censorship and the American Library: The American Library Association's Response to Threats to Intellectual Freedom, 1939–1969* (Greenwood, 1996) 7–8.

10. Brian Quinn, American librarian, in "The McDonaldization of Academic Libraries?," *College and Research Libraries* May 2000: 256.

11. Mary Wright Plummer (1856–1916), American librarian, educator, and 2nd female president of the American Library Association, in her "President's Address: The Public Library and the Pursuit of Truth," delivered at the ALA Annual Conference in Asbury Park, New Jersey, 1916. *Public Libraries* Oct. 1916: 341.

12. Edward Livingston (1764–1836), U.S. Senator and Secretary of State under President Jackson, opposing the Alien & Sedition bills of 1798. This excerpt is extremely paraphrased and can be found in its entirety in the congressional record of June 1798.

13. In a letter to John Wyche, May 19, 1809. *The Writings of Thomas Jefferson* (Taylor & Maury, 1853) 448.

14. Elias Canetti (1905–1994), Bulgarian-born novelist and author of *Auto-da-Fe*, quoted by John Brinkman, "Death of a Bookie," *The Nation* 20 April 1998: 28; a review of Canetti's *Notes from Hampstead: The Writer's Notes: 1954–1971*.

15. "Web Journalism's Sticky Pages," *The Nation* 7 October 2002: 28; review of John Motavalli, *Bamboozled at the Revolution: How Big Media Lost Billions in the Battle for the Internet* (Viking, 2002).

16. John Haar, American librarian, quoted in Theodore Roszak, *The Cult of Information* 2nd ed. (University of California, 1994) 183; quotation is a paraphrase of Haar, "The Politics of Electronic Information: A Reassessment," *Critical Approaches to Information Technology in Librarianship* ed. John Buschman, (Greenwood, 1993) 203,208.

Chapter Eleven: Social Responsibility

1. Robert Wedgeworth, American champion of literacy, library educator, and former executive director of the American Library Association from 1972–1985, in *Library Journal* 1 January 1973, a special issue on the Berninghausen Debate, reprinted in part in "The Berninghausen Debate," *Library Journal* 15 September 1993: S3.

2. Shera 295. (See Note 18, Chapter Two for details.)

3. J. Periam Danton (1908–2002), American library educator author, in "A Plea for a Philosophy of Librarianship," *Library Quarterly* 4:545, October 1934: 545.

4. John Buschman, American librarian and author, in *Dismantling the Public Sphere: Situating and Sustaining Librarianship in the Age of the New Public Philosophy* (Libraries Unlimited, 2003) 109.

5. Quoted in light of the lack of any statement from ALA on the World Trade Organization (WTO) meetings, in contrast to IFLA and the Canadian Library Association, who issued strong statements against the WTO. The ALA sent a delegate to the WTO, but no input from members, or even council for that matter, was solicited, and no report has been made that would inform us about the delegate's participation.

6. From the resolution he proposed to ALA Council in 1999.

7. Frances Clarke Sayers (1897–1989), American librarian, author, critic, storyteller, and educator, in "The Belligerent Profession," *Summoned by Books* ed. Marjeanne Jensen Blinn (Viking, 1965) 28.

8. Kathleen de la Peña McCook, LIS professor and member AFT Local.7463, in her background paper for ALA's Congress on Professional Education titled *Using Ockham's Razor: Cutting to the Center* 3 June 2003, 26 Sept. 2008 <http://librarian.lishost.org/?p=1349>.

9. Found in "For an Organization of Intellectual Workers," *The Einstein Reader* (Citadel, 2006) 163; explaining why he joined the American Federation of Teachers local number 552 as a charter member, 1938.

10. 4 March 2003, 26 Sept. 2008 <http://www.geocities.com/SoHo/Nook/8823/lao_tzu.html>.

11. John Pateman, British librarian, founder and co-editor of *Information for Social Change*, and founder of the Cuban Libraries Solidarity Group, in "Public libraries, social exclusion and social class," *Information for Social Change* Winter 1999–2000, 29 Sept. 2008 <http://www.libr.org/isc/articles/10-public.html>.

12. "Where It's At," *Library Journal* 15 Dec. 1968: .

Chapter Twelve: Neutrality

1. Mark Alfino and Linda Pierce, *Information Ethics for Librarians* (McFarland, 1997) 99.

2. Mark Rosenzweig, co-editor of *Progressive Librarian* and co-founder of the Progressive Librarians Guild, in "Politics and Anti-Politics in Librarianship," *Progressive Librarian* Summer 1991: 3.

3. Chris Atton, British scholar of alternative and community media, in *Alternative Literature: A Practical Guide for Librarians* (Gower, 1996) 170.

4. Victor Navasky (b.1932), American journalism professor and former editor of *The Nation*, in a radio interview by Robert McChesney; *Media Matters*, 15 May 2005, 28 Sept. 2008 <http://rms01.cites.uiuc.edu/ramgen/will/archives/mediamatters050522.rm>.

5. Henry T. Blanke, American reference librarian and co-founder of the Progressive Librarians Guild, in "Librarianship & Political Values: Neutrality or Commitment," *Library Journal* July 1989, 42.

6. Alfino and Pierce, 123. (See Note 1 for details.)

7. "The Fallacy of 'Balance' in Public Library Book Selection," *Library Journal* 1 Feb. 1966: .

8. Jane Robbins, LIS educator and author, in "Social Responsibility and the Library Bill of Rights: The Berninghausen Debate," *Library Journal*, 1 January 1973. Quoted in Alfino and Pierce, 29. (See Note 1 for details.)

9. Celeste West (1942–2008), American librarian, author, and original Revolting Librarian, in "The Library as Motherlode: a Feminist View," In James P. Danky and Elliot Shore, eds., *Alternative Materials in Libraries* (Scarecrow, 1982) 108.

10. Georg Christoph Lichtenberg (1742–1799), German physisist and satarist. in *The Lichtenberg Reader: Selected Writings* trans. Franz H. Mautner and Henry Hatfield (Beacon, 1959) 55.

11. "Minorities Versus Majorities," *Anarchism and Other Essays* (Mother Earth Publishing Association, 1917) 79.

12. Judge Learned Hand (1872–1961), U.S. Court of Appeals judge and judicial philosopher; found in Robertson 161.

13. Paulo Freire (1921–1997), Brazilian educator, in *The Politics of Education: Culture, Power, and Liberation* trans. Donaldo P. Macedo (Greenwood, 1985) 122.

14. Robert Maynard Hutchins (1899–1977), American educator and Editor in Chief of the *Great Books of the Western World* series, in *The Great Conversation* (William Benton, 1952) 80.

Chapter Thirteen: Liberty or Slavery

1. Quoted in Albert Einstein, *The Human Side: New Glimpses from His Archives* eds. Helen Dukas and Banesh Hoffmann (Princeton, 1981) 56.

2. *The Demon-Haunted World: Science as a Candle in the Dark* (Ballantine, 1997) 363.

3. Found on the cover of S. R. Ranganathan's *The Five Laws of Library Science* published by The Madras Library Association, 1931.

4. Bertrand Russell (1872–1970), British philosopher and historian, in *Why Men Fight: A Method of Abolishing the International Duel* (The Century Co., 1917) 179.

5. Frederick Douglas (b. Frederick Augustus Washington Bailey, 1818–1895), American abolitionist, editor, author, and reformer; quoted by Sagan, *Demon-Haunted World* 355.

6. Aldous Huxley (1894–1963), English writer, in *Brave New World Revisited* (Harper & Row, 1965) 96.

7. Epictetus (55–135AD), Greek-born Roman slave & Stoic philosopher, in his *Discourses*, found in *Epictetus: the Discourses as Reported by Arrian the Manual, and Fragments* (Harvard, 1956) 219.

8. Quoted by Albert Bigelow Paine, in "Appendix R: Party Allegience," *Mark Twain: A Biography; the Personal and Literary Life of Samuel Langhorne Clemens* (Harper, 1912) 1665.

9. Thomas Carlyle (1795–1881), Scottish essayist, satirist, and historian, in *Sartor Resartus* ed. Archibald MacMechan (Ginn & Co., 1896) 47.

10. Benjamin Franklin (1706–1790), American Founding Father and polymath; among its many other uses, this was the motto of his *Historical Review of Pennsylvania* (1759). See Richard Frothingham's *The Rise of the Republic of the United States* (Little, Brown, and Company, 1872) 413.

11. George Seldes (1890–1995), American Investigative journalist, in *Lords of the Press* (J. Messner, inc., 1938) 402.

Chapter Fourteen: Truth & Lie

1. "Looking Back at the Spanish War," *Such, Such Were the Joys* (Harcourt, Brace, 1953) 140.

2. Samuel Taylor Coleridge (1772–1834), English poet and critic, in his *Table Talk* entry, June 7 1830. See *Specimens of the Table Talk* (J. Grant, 1905) 96.

3. William Penn (1644–1718), American founding father and founder of the state of Pennsylvania, in *Some Fruits of Solitude* (Kessinger Publishing, 2004) 23.

4. Al Capone (1899–1947), Italian-American gangster and organized crime boss; quoted by George Seldes in *Witch Hunt: The Technique and Profits of Redbaiting* (Modern age books, 1940) 150.

5. Jessica Mitford (1917–1996), British-American author, investigative journalist and member of the Communist Party; quoted by Carl Jensen in *Stories that Changed America: Muckrakers of the 20th Century* (Seven Stories, 2002) 151.

6. Quoted in *Prison Notebooks V.2* ed. Joseph A. Buttigieg (Columbia, 1996) 75.

7. Aeschylus (525–456BC), Greek tragedist; this quotation has been variously attributed to US Senator Hiram Johnson, Arthur Ponsonby, Samuel Johnson, Rudyard Kipling, Aeschylus, and others. See "Who coined the phrase, 'The first casualty of War is Truth'?," *The Guardian UK Online* (date unknown), 27 Sept. 2008 <http://www.guardian.co.uk/notesandqueries/query/0,5753,-21510,00.html>.

8. (Random House, 1976) 157.

9. Mill 17. (See Note 18, Chapter Five for details.)

10. Jean de la Fontaine (1621–1695), French fabulist and poet; quoted by James Wood, ed. *Dictionary of Quotations from Ancient and Modern English and Foreign Sources* (F. Warne and co., 1899) 498.

11. Abraham Lincoln (1809–1865), sixteenth United States president; quoted by Lewis D. Eigen and Jonathan P. Siegel, eds. *The Macmillan Dictionary of Political Quotations* (Macmillan, 1993) 112.

12. George Savile, First Marquess of Halifax (1633–1695), English statesman, writer, and politician; found in *Halifax: Complete Works* ed. John Philipps Kenyon (Penguin Books, 1969) 233.

13. John Locke (1632–1704), English philosopher, in *An Essay Concerning Human Understanding* (Cummings & Hilliard and J. T. Buckingham, 1813) 297.

14. Sigmund Freud (1856–1939), Austrian psychiatrist; quoted in Robertson 132.

Chapter Fifteen: Secrecy

1. Louis Dembitz Brandeis (1856–1941), U.S. Supreme Court Justice, quoted by Richard W. Oliver, *What is Transparency?* (McGraw-Hill, 2004) 50.

2. Patrick Henry (1736–1799), American colonial revolutionary; United States Constitutional Convention, *The Debates in the Several State Conventions on the Adoption of the Federal Constitution, as Recommended by the General Convention at Philadelphia, in 1787* (J.B. Lippincott, 1891) 170.

3. In a letter to Edward Livingston, July 10, 1822. See *The Writings of James Madison* ed. Gaillard Hunt (G.P. Putnam's Sons, 1910) 103.

4. Sissela Bok (b.1934), Swedish philosopher, in *Secrets: On the Ethics of Concealment and Revelation* (Pantheon, 1982) 178–179.

5. Dick Brandon, American computer scientist, systems analyst and author.

6. *Whitney vs. California* 274 U.S. 357 (1927).

7. 1984 (Signet Classic, 1985) 3.

Author Index

A

Achenbach, Joel 139
Aeschylus 121
Agre, Phil 28
Alfino, Mark 109, 111
Allen, Woody 9
Alterman, Eric 135
American Library Association 103
Angus, Ian 142
Atton, Chris 110
Atwood, Margaret 63

B

Bacon, Francis 45
Barber, Lucy 58
Barnett, Lincoln Kinnear 135
Baudrillard, Jean 65
Bauer, Joan 15
Beach, Frederick Converse 135
Bellow, Saul 13
Bentham, Jeremy 56
Berkeley, Sir William 40
Berkman, Alexander 57
Berman, Sanford (Sandy) 26, 33, 37, 39, 49, 103, 106, 141
Berry, John 129–130
Bey, Hakim 24
Billington, James 67, 77

Birkerts, Sven 29
Blanke, Henry 111
Blinn, Marjeanne Jensen 144
Block, Sita 13
Bok, Sissela 127
Bollier, David 61
Borges, Jorge Luis 11
Boswell, James 68
Bowen, Catherine Drinker 81
Bradbury, Ray 76
Bradfield, Bill 132
Brandeis, Louis 125, 127
Brandon, Dick 127
Breen, Marcus 65
Brinkman, John 143
Brittain, Michael 69
Brodsky, Joseph 4
Buffy the Vampire Slayer 86
Buschman, John 102, 144
Buttigieg, Joseph A. 147

C

Cambridge 68
Campbell, Leslie M. 142
Canetti, Elias 95
Capone, Al 121
Carey, Alex 43, 45
Carlyle, Thomas 17, 118

Carnegie, Andrew 17
Carnovsky, Leon 55
Castro, Fidel 7
Cheever, John 131
Chomsky, Noam 42, 47
Coleridge, Samuel Taylor 121
Council of Books in Wartime, The 5
Crawford, Walt 31
Cronkite, Walter 19
Curley, Arthur 129

D

Danky, James 82, 145
Danton, J. Periam 101
DeSirey, Jan 136
Devey, Joseph 136
Dewey, Melvil 39
Dick, Archie L. 90
Dodge, Chris 39, 136
Dogwood, Silence. *See* Franklin, Benjamin
Douglas, Frederick 117
Dukas, Helen 146
Dwyer, Jim 134

E

Eigen, Lewis D. 147
Einstein, Albert 40, 43, 47, 89, 105, 117
Emerson, Ralph Waldo 3
Enron 70
Epictetus 118

F

Farber, Jim 142
Fellner, Gene 138
Finocchiaro, Maurice A. 140
FitzGerald, Tom 130
Flynt, Larry 55
von Foerster, Heinz 66
de la Fontaine, Henri 123
Franklin, Benjamin 118, 137
Freedman, Maurice J. (Mitch) 19, 37, 141
Freire, Paulo 114
Freud, Sigmund 123
Frothingham, Richard 146
Fujiwara, Chris 66
Fuller, Margaret 70

G

Gallagher, Thomas 135
Gandhi 31
y Gasset, José Ortega 85
Gates Jr., Henry Louis 55
Gaunt, Christine 142
Gilbert, G.M. 135
Gillespie, Kerry 134
Gitlin, Todd 76
Goering, Hermann 44
von Goethe, Johann Wolfgang 3
Goldman, Emma 54, 114
Gordon, Thomas 51
Gore, Al 41

Gorman, Michael 54, 132
Gramsci, Antonio 69, 121
Grass, Günther 77
Greenburger, Martin 140
Greer, Germaine 15
Grenier, David 86

H

Haar, John 97
Hand, Learned 114
Harding, Les 137
Hart-Davis, Rupert 139
Hauptman, Robert 28
Hayden, Carla 39
Healy, Timothy 79
Henry, Patrick 127
Herbert, Ann 19
Herman, Edward S. 42
Hoffmann, Banesh 146
Hogard, Lynn 130
Horn, Zoia 38
Humphrey, Hubert H. 53
Hunt, Gaillard 148
Hutchins, Robert Maynard 114
Huxley, Aldous 118

I

Ishizuka, Kathy 138

J

Jast, Louis Stanley 83
Jefferson, Thomas 62, 95, 136
Jensen, Carl 147
Johnson, Hiram 147
Johnson, Samuel 16, 68, 147
Johnson, Steven 76, 139
Johnston, Richard J.H. 130
Jordan, Loretta 19
Joyce, Michael 27

K

Kasdan, Jake 70
Katz, Bill 36
Keillor, Garrison 10, 81
Kelly, Thomas 132
Kennedy, John F. 53
Kenyon, John Philipps 147
Keogh, Andrew 139
Keyes, Ralph 134
King, Martin Luther 13
Kipling, Rudyard 147
Klein, Gary 89
Koch, Theodore 142
Kuhns, William 46
Kundera, Milan 87
Kurtz, Howard 136

L

Lancaster, Frederick W. 142
Landor, Ronald 112
Langton, Jane 14
Lederer, Richard 131
Lessing, Doris 8, 17
Lichtenberg, Georg 70
Lichtenberg, Georg Christoph 114
Lincoln, Abraham 123
Litwin, Rory 131, 136
Livingston, Edward 94, 148
Locke, John 123
Lohrey, Andrew 135

M

MacMechan, Archibald 146
Madison, James 45, 127
Madonna 86
Madras Library Association 117
Magliabecchi, Antonio 85
Mailer, Norman 15
Malcolm X 7, 19
Maraszek, Derek 85
Martinez, Elizabeth 81
McChesney, Robert 145
McCook, Kathleen de la Peña 104
McCrimmon, Barbara 134
McDonald, Peter 38
McGruder, Aaron 56
McPherson, Isaac 139
Mencia, Mario 130

Michaux, Henri 9
Mill, John Stuart 57, 122
Mitford, Jessica 121
Monty Python 20
Moore, Lara Jennifer 40
Moore, Michael 83, 89
Moriarty, Laura 47
Morrone, Francis 67
Motavalli, John 143

N

Navasky, Victor 110
Noam, Eli M. 23
Norman, Melora Ranney 58

O

Oliver, Richard W. 147
Orwell, George 89, 119, 128
Orwell, Sonia 142
Osler, Sir William 8

P

Paine, Albert Bigelow 146
Pateman, John 105
Penn, William 121
Persimmon, E. 48
Peter, Laurence J. 55
Philbin, Regis 83
Pierce, Linda 109, 111
Plummer, Mary Wright 93
Ponsonby, Arthur 147

Author Index

Postman, Neil 26, 30, 32, 65
Pound, Ezra 5
Price, Derek de Solla 86

Q

Quinn, Brian 92

R

Ranganathan, S. R. 146
Raymont, Henry 137
Reed, Sam 91
Reynolds, Sir Joshua 68
Riesman, David 139
Rines, George Edwin 135
Robbins, Jane 113
Robbins, Louise S. 92
Rosenzweig, Mark 109
Rotenberg, Marc 138
Rushdie, Salman 6, 56
rushmc 15
Russell, Bertrand 117

S

Sagan, Carl 57, 67, 117
Savile, George 123
Sayers, Frances Clarke 103
Schiffrin, Andre 41
Schiller, Herbert 35, 90
Schreibman, Vigdor 48
Schuman, Patricia Glass 85
Seldes, George 118, 147

Seneca, Lucius Annaeus 9
de Sevigne, Marie 13
Shakespeare 17
Shera, Jesse 18, 26, 65, 83, 84, 101
Shore, Elliot 145
Siegel, Jonathan P. 147
Siegel, Tatiana 96
Simon, Herbert 75
Starr, Ken 55
Stein, Gertrude 73
Stern, Joseph Peter 140
Stimpson, Catharine R. 140
Stoll, Clifford 4

T

Talbot, Stephen L. 65
Temkin, David 21
Tennant, Roy 61
Thebes, Egypt 15
Thoreau, Henry David 7
Todd, Richard 139
Tomlin, Lily 20
Trelease, Jim 5
Trenchard, John 51
Trevelyan, G.M. 7
troutfishing 86
Twain, Mark 47, 118
Tyson, Mike 7

U

Udall, Morris (Mo) 47
Urgo, Joseph 42, 75
U.S. Supreme Court 57
UUNet 30

V

Vaidhyanathan, Siva 61
Van Impe, Jack 78
Vavrek, Bernard 25
Vidal, Gore 43, 122
Vogel, Jennifer 17
Voltaire 3
Vonnegut, Kurt 67

W

Wagner, Jane 132
Wallace, David Foster 9
Wedgeworth, Robert 99
Weekes, Karen 132
Weeks, Linton 129
Weisbrot, Mark 47
Weizenbaum, Joseph 25
Wertsman, Vladimir 131
West, Celeste 113
Wicker, Tom 136
Wiesel, Elie 13
Wilde, Oscar 55, 67
Willett, Charles 56
Wilson, Bruce 142
Wilson, Peter Lamborn 133

Wood, James 147
Woodward, Kathleen 139
Wyche, John 143

X

XStop 58

Z

Zappa, Frank 71
Zinn, Howard 138

www.ingramcontent.com/pod-product-compliance
Lightning Source LLC
Chambersburg PA
CBHW050907160426
43194CB00011B/2318